NARRATIVE OF THE SUFFERINGS OF LEWIS CLARKE,
DURING A CAPTIVITY OF MORE THAN TWENTY-FIVE YEARS

Narrative of the Sufferings of Lewis Clarke, During a Captivity of More Than Twenty-Five Years, Among the Algerines of Kentucky, One of the So Called Christian States of North America

By Lewis George Clarke

A FACSIMILE EDITION
WITH AN INTRODUCTION
BY CARVER CLARK GAYTON

A V Ethel Willis White Book

UNIVERSITY OF WASHINGTON PRESS   *Seattle and London*

This book is published with the assistance of a grant from
the V Ethel Willis White Endowed Fund, established through
the generosity of Deehan Wyman, Virginia Wyman, and
the Wyman Youth Trust.

The original edition of the Narrative was published in 1845.
First University of Washington Press paperback edition published in 2012
Introduction by Carver Gayton © 2012 by the University of Washington Press
Printed and bound in the United States of America
Design by Thomas Eykemans
16 15 14 13 12   5 4 3 2 1

UNIVERSITY OF WASHINGTON PRESS
PO Box 50096, Seattle, WA 98145, USA
www.washington.edu/uwpress

Library of Congress Control Number: 2012933305

FRONTISPIECE: Lewis Clarke, circa 1890. Family photograph.

Contents

A Re-Introduction to Lewis Clarke, Harriett Beecher Stowe's Forgotten Hero

Carver Clark Gayton

SOME THINK OF HISTORY AS A SUBJECT FOR THE DEAD AND DYING. Others think of it as a false recounting by ideologues. Still others, and I count myself among them, find history a living, breathing, and present entity that provides a compass for the future. I blame my mother.

My father and his side of the family were reluctant to talk about past experiences in Yazoo County, Mississippi, before coming to the Northwest. It was a place and time to move beyond and forget. My father's father left the Deep South never to return, in either word or deed. It was a place of unspoken shame, of slavery and, later, of sharecropping. My grandfather's decision to move to Seattle was progressive and reflected the tone and timbre of many blacks who left the South in the late 1870s, at the end of the Reconstruction Era. The shackles, at least physically, had been broken. Opportunity was waiting for those who took advantage of what he regarded as the American Dream, which would become a reality for him and his future family in Seattle.

My mother, on the other hand, found solace and affirmation in recalling her family's history, which was hardly that of wealth and material success. Her family story was filled with pride and perseverance despite slavery's indelible imprint. She wanted her children to know that no one could diminish the relevance of her decidedly American family, which could trace its roots to the very beginning of the Union.

The family history recounted here follows the links of a colorful and heroic representative of America's fabric from the Revolutionary War to the end of the nineteenth century. It is about a man who faced a tidal wave of American events related to race, which he could have avoided but decided to challenge. The man to whom I refer is Lewis Clarke. He is also known as Lewis Garrard Clarke, Lewis George Clarke, or, most famously, as the man whose early life story was the basis for the character of George Harris in *Uncle Tom's Cabin,* written by Harriet Beecher Stowe.

Gregory Wilson, director of the Sugar Grove Historical Commission in Pennsylvania, was searching the Internet in July 2009 to find information about Lewis George Clarke, my maternal great-grandfather. Clarke, an escaped slave and well-known black abolitionist during the 1840s and 1850s, was the primary source for the storyline of Stowe's classic 1852 novel. Mr. Wilson had read a front-page article in the *Seattle Times* that mentioned my relationship to Clarke.[1] He corresponded with me, wanting information about Clarke's children, one of whom was my grandfather, Cyrus H. Clark. I provided the information and indicated that I would contact him if I discovered anything new. Another communication from the historian referred to an article in the *Washington Post* from May 1890. That extensive coverage indicated that Clarke had been invited to come from Oberlin, Ohio, his home at the time, to speak at the Nineteenth Street Baptist Church in Washington, D.C., about his ventures as well as his memories of Harriet Beecher Stowe.[2]

There was one statement Clarke made in the article that energized me and provided the focus I needed to write about him. Clarke said he was in the process of "getting a book out on his life" and that "after leaving Washington D.C. he would be going to New York and Philadelphia to work out the details." He pointed out that he particularly wanted to correct some of the misleading information that Stowe had in her book.[3] Extensive investigation has not determined whether his planned book was actually ever published. Not having the written story of his life from his perspective, we—the family and the public—are less fortunate as a result. I hope that this publication about his exciting and memorable life helps to some degree to fulfill my great-grandfather's wish.

CHILDHOOD RECOLLECTIONS IN SEATTLE
OF THE FAMILY TREE

While my father was the center of attention during dinnertime, my mother "held court" most evenings. This was a time set aside for family bonding.

I also believe Mom wanted us to feel secure during the war years. From 1941 through 1945, deafening air raid sirens in Seattle would be sounded, often after dark, and we would draw down the black shades to ensure lights from our home could not be seen by air. Air raid wardens, like my dad and my brother John, would don their white steel helmets and scour their assigned sections of the neighborhood to check that all the shades were drawn and to direct people to leave the streets. I was frightened by the sirens and visualized Japanese fighter planes swooping down on our house. That fear was more than justified during the uncertain first two years of the war because of the clear threat posed by the Japanese military. I had terrible nightmares of the war from the ages of three to seven. The stories Mom read consoled me and helped take my mind off the war.

The stories I enjoyed included those about King Arthur's court, *Treasure Island* by Robert Lewis Stevenson, Joel Chandler Harris's *Uncle Remus* (based on folklore of African slaves), and all the traditional children's fairy tales. While she read, the radio was turned off. Very few families had television in Seattle at the time. I especially enjoyed those evenings when Mom would ask us questions from the latest issue of *Parent's Magazine*. I enjoyed the challenge of those sessions but hated being wrong. If I missed an answer, I couldn't wait for the opportunity to be correct on the next one.

Invariably the family gatherings led to discussions of Negro leaders of the past. Some of them included the great poet Phillis Wheatley, who once was invited to President George Washington's home so that he could personally thank her for a poem; inventor and architect Benjamin Banneker, whose city plans of Washington, D.C., were utilized as the model for the current configuration of the nation's capital[4]; abolitionist Frederick Douglass, confidant of Presidents Lincoln, Grant, and Garfield; educator and political leader Booker T. Washington; National Association for the Advancement of Colored People (NAACP) founder W. E. B. DuBois; black nationalist Marcus Garvey; scientist George Washington Carver; as well as U.S. Patent Office attorney Henry Baker, chronicler of Negro inventors of the nineteenth century.

Talking about Baker was especially fun because he was my mother's uncle. She resided at his home in the 1920s when she attended Howard University in Washington, D.C. Baker married Violetta Clark, one of the daughters of Lewis G. Clarke. Violetta, grandfather Cyrus Clark's sister, was a librarian at the U.S. Library of Congress and completed her librarianship program at Amherst College in Massachusetts.

Few if any of these outstanding contributors to American science, culture, and the arts were ever discussed in the schools that I and my siblings attended, but they were referenced in books during evening conversations with my mother and, from time to time, my father. Always included in these discussions of black leaders was Mom's grandfather, Lewis Garrard Clarke, African American hero and colleague of Frederick Douglass. From the bookcase in our living room, she would pull out a careworn volume with a plum red cover entitled *The Key to Uncle Tom's Cabin,* by Harriet Beecher Stowe. I would learn later that the book was written in response to detractors of *Uncle Tom's Cabin* who were convinced that the storyline regarding the harsh treatment of slaves was an exaggeration. *The Key* provided examples of real experiences of slaves. My mother would turn to the chapter on George Harris, a lead character in *Uncle Tom's Cabin*, who was described as a rebellious runaway slave with white features. We learned that Lewis G. Clarke was the real-life individual upon whom George Harris was based.

My brothers and sisters never tired of hearing the stories about great-grandfather Clarke. As a child, I did not believe that his adventures were anything more than interesting family folklore. I later learned that he risked his life assisting blacks' escape from slavery. He went further by speaking out against slavery's evils in public forums across the northern states and Canada before the beginning of the Civil War. After the war and until his death, he was invited to speak throughout the nation about his experiences as a slave and about the ongoing challenges facing freed slaves. To this day I continue to be impressed by his bravery and commitment to the civil and human rights of African Americans. It was not until much later in life, after greater appreciation of history and considerable research, that I realized that he was also a hero and patriot.

LEWIS G. CLARKE

The more I discovered about the life of Lewis Clarke, the more fascinated I became. His father, Daniel Clarke, a Scotsman, fought at Bunker Hill and continued in the army until the end of the Revolutionary War.[5] Lewis Clarke's grandfather, Samuel Campbell, a slave master, was also a Scotsman. He served as a captain for three years during the Revolutionary War in Bedford County, Virginia, and was at Yorktown, as was Clarke, when the British surrendered to General George Washington in 1781.[6] That I can trace my family's roots in this country to colonial times gives me considerable pride. As a recent inductee into the National Society, Sons of the American Revolution, I enjoy attending the local NSSAR meetings and reminding my "compatriots" that not only did people with African bloodlines have a role in the War of Independence, but also that the descendants of many others who fought had African bloodlines. My great-grandfather's story reflects a continuum of more than 230 years of my family's commitment to human rights issues in America. My story is even more unusual in that I am the descendant of both slaves *and* slave owners.

A gravestone in Westwood Cemetery in Oberlin, Ohio, reads "Lewis G. Clarke, March 1815–December 1897, The Original George Harris of Harriet Beecher Stowe's Book, *Uncle Tom's Cabin.*" The real-life stories of Lewis Clarke and his nine brothers and sisters, from which Harriet Beecher Stowe used most of the incidents for the plot of *Uncle Tom's Cabin*, are even more dramatic than those in the fictional account. Lewis captured the details in his book *Narrative of the Sufferings of Lewis Clarke, During a Captivity of More than Twenty-Five Years, Among the Algerines of Kentucky, One of the So Called Christian States of North America*, published in April 1845 and reproduced here in its entirety more than 165 years later. This was written before the most well-known African American abolitionist, Frederick Douglass, published *Narrative of the Life of Frederick Douglass, an American Slave* later that year. The men knew each other, and many historical references are made of Clarke and Douglass lecturing before the Civil War at the same forums in Massachusetts and New York on behalf of the American Anti-Slavery Society. Clarke's book was dictated to Joseph C. Lovejoy, a minister in Cambridge, Massachusetts, who was active in abolitionist causes in the Northeast. Many copies of Clarke's book were sold, but it created so much excitement in the Northeast that several thousand copies were suppressed and the plates destroyed. Few original copies are in existence today.[7] In 1846, a subsequent book was published entitled *Narratives of the Sufferings of Lewis and Milton Clarke, Sons of a Soldier of the Revolution*, which included Lewis's brother's experiences as a slave. Fundamentally, there was little difference between the books.[8] The primary change was the addition of a series of questions and answers regarding slavery in the appendix.

Lewis's saga begins with his mother, Letitia, or "Letty" Campbell, born out of wedlock to Samuel Campbell, a wealthy Kentucky plantation owner.[9] Her mother, Mary, was Campbell's mulatto slave. Campbell later legally married another Mary, Mary Anderson Kennedy. Letty grew up as a slave in the Campbell household with white half brothers and sisters. According to a granddaughter of Samuel Campbell, Mary Ann Banton, Letty was regarded as an "especial favorite" of the Campbell family.[10]

When the War of 1812 commenced, Campbell went to the front and left his wife and children at home with an easier mind knowing of "Letitia's faithfulness and capability" as a house servant. Before Campbell left he hired a "humbler countryman," a Scotsman, to be the family weaver. A year went by and Campbell returned home. He was told by his wife that the weaver, Daniel Clarke, and Letitia had become lovers. Campbell ordered Clarke off the plantation and lectured Letitia that terrible things would happen to both of them if they brought scandal upon his name. Campbell left again for the war for a short period of time, and found Clarke still on the estate when he returned home.

Another scene took place:

> He threatened to cowhide Clarke who bade him to do as he pleased because he loved Letitia.
>
> 'Hoot, toot, man!' exclaimed Campbell. 'You're a grand fool. Do you suppose I want a lot of white negro children on my place? And don't you know your children will be my slaves—that I will put them in my pocket—that I will sell them?'
>
> But nothing daunted Clarke, and he married Letitia, vowing her master would never sell her children.[11]

Having lost his first wife, with whom he had two sons, in Scotland, Daniel Clarke came to this country to fight with the Colonists.[12] A wounded veteran of the Revolutionary War, he fought in major campaigns in the Northeast and possibly Virginia. Research indicates that Clarke may have fought as a Minuteman and marched to Cambridge on the alarm of April 19, 1775, with Col. William Prescott's regiment, which went on to fight in the Battle of Bunker Hill in June 1775.[13]

One can appreciate Daniel's bravery not only for his actions as a soldier but also for marrying a slave, considering the social mores of that time. Letty bore Daniel nine children, with Lewis being the seventh. Daniel was eventually assured by Samuel Campbell that Letty and any of the children born to her would be granted freedom in Campbell's will. It was with this promise that Daniel married her; however, that promise was never fulfilled. The only semblance of family life for the Clarkes was during the early lives of the children. Letty served as the cook in her father's house. Daniel, homesick for Scotland and its legends, often sang folksongs of his native land. Lewis was taught how to spin flax by his father and utilized this skill for work as well as entertainment his entire life. Even though the family was together for a time, their lives were fragile. Given that the children were the legitimate offspring of a free white father and a quadroon mother, the likelihood of their becoming free would have seemed greater. Nevertheless, they remained in slavery.

When Samuel Campbell died in 1821, Lewis was six years old.[14] The will within which he promised the freedom of Letitia and her children was never found. More than likely it was found and destroyed by Campbell's heirs. The market value of slaves was probably too tempting to disregard.

Letty and her children were included in the assets of the estate, in spite of the angry interference of one of the daughters, Judith Campbell Logan. "Letty is our own half-sister and you know it," she protested to her brothers and sisters. "You know Father never meant that she and her children *should* be sold." Daniel Clarke, now old and ill, was outraged. Having fought for his country's freedom from British rule, he said bitterly, "Must I now see my wife and children sold in this free country?"[15] Lewis's father was apparently helpless to stop his wife and children from being sold. Pleas from both Daniel Clarke and Judith Logan were ignored. The auction proceeded, and mother and children were sold at prices ranging from $300 to $800 and relocated to different plantations, primarily in Kentucky.

Lewis was separated from his mother and siblings to become the slave of Betsy Campbell Banton, Samuel Campbell's daughter, and her husband John.[16] In the ten years he spent with the Bantons, he was allowed to see his family only three times. He described that period of his life as his most miserable and loneliest. He suffered constant beatings and whippings from Mrs. Banton. Her tools of torture were usually the raw hide or a bunch of hickory sprouts seasoned by fire and tied together.

Lewis began, by the age of nine, to spin flax and hemp. He worked from dawn to dusk. Being exhausted by the end of each day made it impossible for him to stay awake, and at such times Mrs. Banton would throw dippers full of vinegar and salt into his sleepy eyes. Lewis pointed out in his narrative that "Mrs. Banton, as is common among slave holding women, seemed to hate and abuse me all the more because I had the blood of her father in my veins." Additionally, her husband was known to drive hot nails into the back of a slave who worked in the blacksmith shop who on occasion displeased him.

Lewis witnessed even more horrendous treatment of slaves outside of the Banton plantation. He watched as a runaway slave named Tom was caught by an overseer and whipped three-hundred lashes. Lewis described how he had the job of washing Tom's back with salt and water. He said, "It was the hardest work I ever did. The flesh would crawl, and creep, and quiver under my hands."[17] Slave owners initiated this approach to whippings, according to Lewis, in order to make the slaves "smart," that is, make it painful enough so the slave would think twice before committing other rebellious actions and also to prevent "mortification" (infection) in the lacerated flesh.

The worst kind of torture Lewis witnessed in Kentucky was seeing a slave woman stripped naked and hung up by her hands and whipped until blood ran down her back. This act was even more degrading when it was done by a young master or mistress to an aged mother, or even a grandmother. Clarke said, "Nothing the slaves abhor as they do this."[18]

A poignant and heartbreaking story heard and witnessed by abolitionist Lydia Maria Child in 1842 was recounted by Clarke in many of his lectures and speeches for the American Anti-Slavery Society:

> Preacher Raymond didn't used to flog his slaves; he used to duck' em. He had a little slave girl, about eight years old, that he used to duck very often. One day, the family went to a meeting, and left her to take care of a young child. The child fretted, and she thought she would serve it as master served her; so she ducked it, and it slipped out of her hands and got drowned. They put her in prison, and sentenced her to be hung; but she, poor child, didn't know nothing at all what it meant. When they took her to the gallows, she was guarded all round by men, but she was so innocent, she didn't know what they were going to do with her. She stooped to pick up a pin, and stuck it in her frock, as she went. The poor young thing was so glad to get out of prison that she was as merry as if she was going to her mother's house."[19]

The above are examples of the degradation, humiliation, and pain that Clarke and other slaves endured or witnessed while in bondage. Harriet Beecher Stowe compared the slave experiences of Clarke and Frederick

Douglass in her book *Key to Uncle Tom's Cabin,* and stated that "the case of Lewis Clarke's [experience as a slave] is a harder one than common [within slavery]. The case of [Frederick] Douglass is probably a very fair average specimen."[20]

In Clarke's written narration and lectures, he presented his stories with a unique blend of sarcasm, bitterness, pathos, and comedy. All of those characteristics are reflected in his anecdote of the slave named George:

> A slave, named George, was the property of a man of high standing in the church. The old gentleman was taken sick, and the doctor told him he would die. He called George, and told him if he would wait upon him attentively, and do everything for him possible, he would remember him in his will: he would do something handsome for him.
>
> George was very much excited to know what it might be; hoped it might be in the heart of his master to give him his freedom. At last, the will was made. George was still more excited. The master noticed it, and asked what the matter was. "Massa, you promise to do something for me in your will. Poor nigger! What massa done for George?" "O George, don't be concerned; I have done a very handsome thing for you—such as any slave would be proud to have done for him." This did not satisfy George. He was still very eager to know what it was. At length the master saw it necessary to tell George, to keep him quiet, and make him attend to his duty. "Well, George, I have made provision that, when you die, you shall have a good coffin, and be put into the same vault with me. Will not that satisfy you, George?" "Well, massa, one way I am satisfied, and one way I am not." "What, what," said the old master, "what is the matter with that?" "Why," says George, "I like to have good coffin when I die." "Well, don't you like to be in the same vault with me and other rich masters?" "Why, yes, massa, one way I like it, and one way I don't." "Well, what don't you like?" "Why, I 'fraid, massa, when de debbil come take you body, he make mistake, and get mine."[21]

Clarke observed that slaves preferred to be buried at the greatest possible distance from their masters. They were, according to Clarke, superstitious and feared that the slave drivers, having whipped them so much when alive, would somehow beat them when dead.

In 1833 Letty Clarke died of cholera.[22] Daniel Clarke had died approximately six years before.[23] It was around the time of his father's death that

Lewis Clarke was sold by the Banton family because of financial difficulties resulting from John Banton's involvement in a counterfeiting plot. Lewis's new master was General Thomas Kennedy, of Garrard County, Kentucky.

Thomas Kennedy, who fought in the War of Independence, came to Kentucky in about 1780, fighting Indians along the way. Kennedy ultimately owned seven thousand acres of land and one hundred and fifty slaves.[24] He was enormously wealthy in those days. Clarke referred to Kennedy as Mr. K in his 1845 narrative because of fear that "he or any other man should ever claim *property* where they never had any."[25] His situation improved greatly compared to what he experienced under the Bantons. Although he had more freedom and less cruelty, it was "far from enviable."[26] For example, the whipping death of Uncle Tom in Harriet Beecher Stowe's book was suggested by the fate of Sam Peter, a blacksmith on General Kennedy's plantation who, because of a small offence, was swung up by his hands to the limbs of a locust tree by Kennedy, an overseer, and a waiter. He was whipped in turn by each with several hundred lashes. Two months later he was dead. Clarke heard him say to his mother, in words almost identical to those used by Old Tom: "Mother, tell master he has killed me at last for nothing, but tell him if God will forgive him, I will."[27] Clarke asserted that the character of Uncle Tom in Stowe's book was based upon the experiences of three slaves: Sam Peter, J. Banton of Kentucky, and Reverend Josiah Henson. All were acquaintances of Clarke. The character of the evil Simon Legree was based in part on the life of Thomas Kennedy.[28]

In 1836 Thomas Kennedy died, and after the division of his estate, Lewis Clarke became the slave of Thomas Kennedy Jr., the general's son. The young Kennedy found it more profitable to hire out Lewis's time. This meant he would board and clothe himself and turn whatever he earned back to his master. He was allowed to travel around on horseback with an open pass, selling grass seed, splitting rails, and trading and weaving, paying his master a certain sum a month. For Lewis, this new situation gave him an even greater desire to be free.

After the death of young Kennedy in 1840, Lewis heard rumors that he might be sold and sent to Louisiana by the administrators of the estate, Judge John Letcher, the son-in-law of General Kennedy, and a Mr. Bridges. Louisiana was regarded as one of the states that treated slaves the worst. It was at this time that Clarke decided to make his break for freedom. In an

1881 interview, Mrs. Nancy Letcher, the wife of John Letcher, described the last days Clarke was on the plantation:

> It happened in this way. My bother Tom, Lewis' master, died and Lewis was seized with fear that he would be sold and taken south. There was little authority for his fears. My husband and my brother-in-law, Mr. Bridges, were the administrators of my brother's estate. They found out that a sale would have to take place, and in talking the matter over one day in the house they were overheard by some nurse girls [slaves], who immediately reported it to the cabins. Lewis heard it and was greatly frightened. . . . The dread of life in the South then was the greatest felt by any Kentucky Negro. Lewis, to avoid the supposed fate, ran away. He still kept his pass, and was enabled to reach the [Ohio] river by means of it. He afterwards in a letter confessed it to me.
>
> I believe, indeed, I surprised him with his preparations. Although he had a wife, he had his washing done by one of the women who was a servant about the house. He was very particular about his toilet. I have supposed that his wife could not please him in that regard. One morning I got up a little earlier than usual, and stepping out of my room, saw Lewis passing by, holding a bundle in his hands. I asked him what he held. He replied "Nothing, ma'm, but my clean shirts," and passed on in the direction of his cabin. I afterwards learned that he was gone, and I have no doubt that the bundle he was carrying was part of the preparation for his journey.[29]

No mention was made in Clarke's narrative of having been married or of leaving a wife and child behind. Mrs. Letcher, however, indicated that Lewis had a wife named Margy and that they had a beautiful child named Elmada. But Lewis took neither with him, and he did not make any effort to have them join him. Mrs. Letcher stated, "From a letter he sent me some time afterwards, it appeared that he had forgotten them entirely."[30] In an August 1896 article, a house boy of Mrs. Letcher's brother, Norman Kennedy, indicates that he knew Lewis Clarke well. He verifies Mrs. Letcher's account regarding Clarke's relationship with Margy, although he called her Maggie.[31] He said that Maggie was left behind, but soon ran off to Louisville with her child. "She secreted herself in Falls City [Louisville] until Clarke returned from Ohio. She joined him there and the two went up the Ohio River by steam boat to Cincinnati." Maggie was the Eliza in Mrs. Stowe's novel and the wife of George Harris (Lewis Clarke).[32] Stowe described Eliza's dramatic escape across the drifting ice of the Ohio River from Kentucky to Ohio and freedom. In August 1880 a Chicago reporter asked Clarke if he had any recollection of whom Eliza could have been. He replied "There was such a woman. She crossed the Ohio in 1841—the same winter I was in Oberlin. The river was full of floating cakes of ice at the time. She left one of the child's garments on the bank, so those seeing it would think that she and the child were drowned. I knew Levi Coffin [a Quaker abolitionist] and his wife Catherine, who gave her a change of clothing and cared for her after she landed."[33] No references to a Margy or Maggie were ever made by Clarke during his lifetime despite eyewitness accounts to the contrary.

In August 1841, Clarke and another slave named Isaac started north from Garrard County, Kentucky, on horseback. Because of Clarke's light skin, they tried to pose as master and body servant. In *Uncle Tom's Cabin,* George Harris used this ruse to escape, but in real life Clarke had gone only a few miles with his friend when they realized that their inability to read signposts and their awkward manners would reveal them. They returned, and two weeks later Lewis set out alone on a horse. The first night he stayed with his brother Cyrus in Lexington, Kentucky. The next day he continued on and by nightfall reached the village of Mayslick, twenty miles from the Ohio River and freedom. Tired because of the day's journey and fearful of being recognized, he debated his choices. If he entered the nearby tavern he could be recognized; if he slept in the fields, roving dogs could detect him. With a pair of green spectacles as a disguise, he braved the tavern and spent a fearful and sleepless night.[34]

At dawn he was on his way, and by noon he crossed the Ohio River. Lewis Clarke stood on free soil at last. He was safe. His goal was to reach Canada. His major challenge was not to disclose himself as an escaped slave during the journey north.

Making cautious and discrete inquiries, he sold his horse and boarded a canal boat at Portsmouth, Ohio, and headed for Cleveland. He remained in Cleveland for several days, not knowing for sure how to get across Lake Erie to Canada. He had a hard time conceiving the fact that Canada was really there. He was also concerned that his questions could lead to suspicion. He listened until he heard of a ship bound for Port Stanley, Ontario, and booked passage. When he stepped ashore he could say at last,

"I AM FREE. . . . Not till *then*, did I dare to cherish for a moment the feeling that *one* of the limbs of my body, was my own. . . . My hands, my feet, were now my own. But what to do with them was the next question. A strange sky was over me, a new earth under me, strange voices all around. . . . I was entirely alone; no human being that I had ever seen before, where I could speak to him or he to me."[35]

For a period of time fear and loneliness consumed him. Kentucky slave holders had told their slaves that Canadians would blind runaways and force them to work in the coal mines. They said the "redcoats" would skin the heads of escaped slaves and wear the wool around their necks for collars.

Lewis's brother Milton had made his way to Canada months earlier. Lewis searched the area to find him. In Chatham he saw a sight that finally diminished his fears: two black soldiers driving before them a white prisoner with his hands bound. Finally he met an old friend named Henry, who told him that Milton had gone back to Oberlin, Ohio. Lewis then crossed from Sandwich, Ontario, to Detroit. Low in funds, he boarded a steamer destined for Cleveland and told the captain of his financial plight, convincing him to take him on credit. While in Cleveland he sold his hair brush and overcoat to pay for food, lodging, and stage fare to Oberlin.

In Oberlin at last he found Milton living at a boarding house of a Mrs. Cole. Mrs. Cole and many of her friends were active in the abolitionist movement. Lewis had not seen Milton in over a year, and the brothers were extremely happy to see each other. Milton spoke of going to Massachusetts. Lewis was not enthusiastic about his proposal, indicating that it would be safer to stay in Oberlin, with its large numbers of abolitionists. Milton assured him that in Massachusetts the abolitionists were more numerous than in Ohio.[36]

Lewis's more immediate plan was to rescue his younger brother Cyrus from slavery in Kentucky. He did not tell more than one or two people in Oberlin of his intentions. He may not have even mentioned it to Milton. He left Oberlin in July 1842, destined for Kentucky. After much intrigue Lewis ultimately connected with Cyrus at his home in Lexington, where Lewis was concealed in a small room for a week. Cyrus's wife, who was a freed slave, helped prepare both men for the exhausting trip on foot to the north. Lewis decided that they would not take horses because if they were caught, the penalty for stealing horses would be far worse than the charge of running away. Finally getting across the Ohio River to Ripley, Ohio, Cyrus in his exultation, flung himself on the grass and cried out that this was the first time "he ever rolled on *free* grass."[37] Friends helped them to get to Oberlin, where they stayed for a few days. The dangerous mission took a total of five weeks from the time Lewis left Oberlin and returned. Cyrus went on to Canada. After arriving there he sent a letter to his wife in Lexington advising her of his safety. A short time later, Cyrus went back to the states, joining his wife, who had come north and then east to Hamilton, New York.

In August 1842, while in Oberlin, Lewis and Milton had a close encounter with two bounty hunters who were employed by Deacon Archibald Logan in Kentucky, the owner of Milton.[38] They attempted to take Milton back to Kentucky, but several citizens of the town hindered them, and they were sent back to Kentucky empty handed. This experience convinced Lewis and Milton to move to the Northeast, with Lewis going to New York City and Milton to Cambridge, Massachusetts.[39] Lewis had made contact with a powerful leader in the abolitionist movement, philanthropist Lewis Tappan (1788–1873), who was interested in his exploits as a slave. Lewis had brought to Tappan letters from Ohio that certified his experiences as a slave. Those who wrote the letters were friends of Tappan and probably met him through Tappan's association with Oberlin College, where he had donated large sums of money. At that time, Oberlin was the only college in the nation that admitted blacks and women. Tappan was also a founder of the American Anti-Slavery Society, along with William Lloyd Garrison. Tappan hired attorneys, including former U.S. President John Quincy Adams, to defend the illegally enslaved Africans of the slave ship *Amistad*.[40] The case was won on appeal to the Supreme Court of the United States in 1839. This case was the most significant regarding slavery in U.S. history up to that time. It was eclipsed by the Dred Scott decision in 1857, which determined unequivocally that Negroes were not citizens of the United States and had no rights, as such, anywhere in the nation.

Lewis stayed for about a week with Tappan and continued connecting with elite company in New York. Noted abolitionist Lydia Maria Child (1802–1880) was informed by Tappan that Clarke was speaking to an audience in Brooklyn, and Tappan suggested that she listen to his fascinating story. Tappan introduced Clarke at the October 20, 1842, meeting. At the end of Clarke's presentation regarding what he endured as a slave, Tappan told Child that a slave owner from Mississippi was in attendance who said afterwards that "he heard nothing incredible [from Clarke]. He says he is going to emancipate his slaves forthwith." Tappan added, "God give him the grace to keep his word."[41]

Lewis Clarke went to Cambridge in December 1842, where he became even more active in abolitionist causes. He helped other slaves escape from the South and lectured extensively throughout the Northeast. In 1843 he met Joseph C. Lovejoy, the Congregational pastor to whom he dictated *Narrative of the Sufferings of Lewis Clarke*. Lovejoy was impressed, particularly with Clarke's intelligence and integrity. Clarke's *Narrative* was initially published as a pamphlet and sold at abolitionist meetings in 1843. A hardback edition was published in 1845.

John Blassingame states in his 2001 introduction to *Narrative of the Life of Frederick Douglass* that

> between 1838 and 1845, Douglass avidly read . . . speeches, interviews, and autobiographies of dozens of fugitive slaves including Lunsford Lane, James Curry, Lewis Clarke, and the *Amistad* rebels. Equally significant, the abolitionist newspapers and magazines published reviews of the autobiographies of blacks and whites and furnished Douglass with further advice on the elements of the proper autobiography.[42]

Douglas held Clarke in such high esteem that he named his son Lewis after Clarke.[43]

THE HARRIET BEECHER-STOWE CONNECTION

While in Cambridge, Clarke stayed nearly seven years with Aaron Safford, a Boston merchant, and his wife, Mary, step-daughter of Lyman Beecher, Harriet Beecher Stowe's father. Mrs. Stowe oddly and obliquely refers to Mary in *Key to Uncle Tom's Cabin* by pointing out that Clarke was "received into the family of a sister-in-law of the author, and there educated. His conduct during this time was such as to win for him uncommon affection and respect, and the author has frequently heard him spoken of in the highest terms by all who knew him. The gentleman [Safford] in whose family he so long resided, says of him, in a recent letter to the writer, 'I would trust him, as the saying is, with untold gold.'"[44] Clarke often remarked that Mary Jackson Safford "taught me more than anyone else." Stowe described Clarke as follows: "Lewis is a quadroon [octoroon], a fine-looking man, with European features, hair slightly wavy, and with an intelligent, agreeable expression of countenance." Why Stowe did not mention Mrs. Safford's name or elaborate upon her relationship with Lewis Clarke perhaps suggests a personal conflict with her or concern about copyright issues regarding the storyline of *Uncle Tom's Cabin*.

Lewis and Milton joined the Second Evangelical Congregational Church in Cambridge, pastored by Reverend Lovejoy. Lewis's fame rose during his time in the town thanks to the publication of his two narratives. Mary Jackson Safford arranged for Lewis to meet Harriet Beecher Stowe in 1844, which led to several interviews with Lewis in the Safford home. Lewis pointed out that "Mrs. Stowe visited there on purpose to hear my story. She used to send for me to come to the parlor and talk with me for hours at a time about my experiences as a slave."[45] He went on to say that Mrs. Stowe took full notes of all that he told her. In May 1881, when Clarke was sixty-five, he was asked by a reporter how Harriet Beecher Stowe came to write her classic novel. Clarke replied:

> Dr. [Gamaliel] Bailey, who published *The Philanthropist* in Cincinnati, had been persuaded to move to Washington City [Washington, D.C.] about 1848 or 1850, where he established an emancipationist organ, *The National Era*.
>
> When the fugitive slave law was passed [1850] it produced such an impression upon the country, and was so strongly sustained by the press and even the pulpit, that the emancipationists were paralyzed for some time. *The National Era* lost circulation steadily, and was on the point of extinction, when Dr. Bailey went to New York to consult with some leading emancipationists as to what course he should pursue. He thought he could get some woman of literary reputation and ability to write a series of articles for his paper every week on the subject of slavery and its violation of the finest sentiments, that it would receive public interest and carry his paper to people it had never reached before. The names of Lydia M. Child and others were proposed but not accepted. Lewis Tappan, who was one of the counselors, finally said he knew of one woman who could do the work successfully; that she was poor and must be paid for it, but that she would succeed. He then mentioned Mrs. Stowe, and advised Dr. Bailey to write her, and by way of earnest, inclose (*sic*) her a draft for $100. The letter was written and the draft sent. The next week there appeared in the columns of *The National Era*, not the first of a series of articles on slavery, but the first chapters of a story

called *Uncle Tom's Cabin*. The effect was instantaneous and great. Circulation of *The National Era* was increased at once, and soon became very large. Mrs. Stowe was poor and earning her money so laboriously that for fear the great novel would be cut short she was sent an additional draft for $300. Then she copyrighted the story, which became more famous than any novel ever issued from a printing press.

The reporter who interviewed Clarke added unequivocally, "Into the book she wove all the facts given her by Lewis Clarke, in connection with the information gleaned elsewhere."[46]

It is thus very plausible that the writing of the great novel did not come about by happenstance. It was, in Clarke's opinion, a clearly orchestrated plan on the part of abolitionist leaders, with Lewis Tappan at the forefront. Documented history shows that Tappan played similar roles for other significant events related to the abolitionist movement, and Clarke could certainly have been in the middle of the machinations because he knew most if not all of the main players and his story was a powerful contribution for the abolitionist cause. Clarke unabashedly pointed out in an 1890 *Washington Post* interview that "if she had not gotten acquainted with me, she [Stowe] never could have written that book in her life, for she would not have been able to get the information."[47] As previously indicated, Stowe acknowledged in *Key to Uncle Tom's Cabin* that she had been acquainted with Clarke and that his experience as a slave was the basis for George Harris, a major character in the novel. Young E. Allison, a highly respected reporter for the *Louisville Courier*, stated that "the book which Lewis Clarke aided in producing (and nobody who reads his *Narrative* can doubt where Mrs. Stowe got most of her facts and suggestions) . . . created a situation where black children in 1881 were learning to read and write in rural Lowell, Kentucky which in all *probability* could not have happened without the publication of the book."[48] Stowe, however, never indicated that Clarke influenced her to the extent that he and many others asserted. As Allison suggested, a reading of Clarke's 1845 narrative clearly reflected a likeness to the broad themes and major characters of the 1852 *Uncle Tom's Cabin*. As the years passed and Lewis Clarke's connection with *Uncle Tom's Cabin* became more widely known, Harriet Beecher Stowe and her heirs incredulously objected that Stowe had never met Clarke and that his claims to being the model for George Harris were completely false. In 1895, a Maysville, Kentucky, newspaper reported:

Harriet Beecher Stowe has written a letter to Lexington parties in which she says, "The man you speak of, George Lewis Clarke, who is going about representing himself to be the original George in *Uncle Tom's Cabin*, does so at his own presumption. I never saw the man, and don't remember ever having even heard of him, although I have before received letters telling of various individuals who were going about the country representing themselves to be the originals of Uncle Tom, or George Harris, as the case might be. Neither he nor any other man stood for the character of George Harris, who was a creature of my own brain—a probable but not living character."[49]

Narrative of the Sufferings of Lewis Clarke was the first book ever copyrighted by a slave. That in itself reflects the importance of the publication in the eyes of abolitionist leaders who were mentoring Clarke after his escape from slavery. It was Clarke's vivid descriptions in his book of the harsh cruelties of slave life that captured the attention of the public. Harriet Beecher Stowe herself stated that what Clarke endured and witnessed while in captivity was considerably worse than what Frederick Douglass experienced, as well as that of many other slaves.[50] One of Clarke's major criticisms of Stowe was that she failed to reflect in *Uncle Tom's Cabin* the essence of the evils of slave life that he passed on to her during their many conversations.[51]

Although Stowe revealed in *Key to Uncle Tom's Cabin* that the character George Harris *was* based upon the experiences of Lewis Clarke, she implied that her connection with Clarke was cursory and insignificant. If in fact she met with him over a period of years, taking notes during each visit, and knew of the publication of his book, which was advertised in *The National Era,* where she worked, she was more than likely encouraged to talk with Clarke through their mutual mentor Lewis Tappan. Questions are raised as to why Stowe wanted to dismiss the importance of her affiliation with Clarke and why Stowe's biographers never elaborated upon her relationship with Lewis Tappan, and discussions on these matters necessitate further research.

Clarke's unique story had much more of an impact on creating the framework for *Uncle Tom's Cabin* than her biographers were willing or able to admit. Newspaper writers (e.g., Teamoh, Allison, and Fuller) reported for years after the publication that if one read Clarke's *Narrative* and then Stowe's novel, no one would doubt that the storyline of her masterpiece came from Clarke's book. Assuming the veracity of Clarke's assertions makes the significance of Clarke's *Narrative* that much more important in the annals of American history. In the nineteenth century, *Uncle Tom's Cabin* was the second best-selling book after the Bible. In 1853, 300,000 copies were sold in the United States and 2 million copies around the world.[52] It is indisputably one of the most popular novels ever written and one of the most important works of literary propaganda ever written. It was crucial in swaying citizens in the Northern states to oppose slavery and therefore to back Abraham Lincoln and the Union in the war against the Confederacy. Lincoln was not being condescending when he first met Stowe after the beginning of the war and purportedly said, "So you are the little woman who started this great war."

When Lewis Clarke died in December 16, 1897, neither the state of Kentucky nor the nation forgot his contributions to his country. He was the first African American to lie in state in Kentucky's capital, Lexington. Full-page stories of his funeral and his life appeared in publications throughout the nation and the world, with headlines such as "Lewis Clarke, An Historic Negro, Remarkable Career Ends," "Honored for the Part He Played in Making History," and "A Figure in History: The Career of the Late Lewis Clarke."

One may ask why I decided to initiate another publication of the 1845 *Narrative*. I must admit that a driving interest is very personal, in that Clarke is my maternal great-grandfather and I want to honor him. But more importantly, neither my immediate family nor the general public is aware of his significant contributions to the abolitionist movement and ultimately to the elimination of the "peculiar institution" of slavery.

As I began writing, my primary focus was on publishing a family history. As my research regarding my ancestors evolved, I became almost overwhelmed by all of the material I was finding on Lewis Clarke. At that point I decided to focus my energies exclusively on Clarke and his impact on the historical landscape of America. Literally hundreds of books, manuscripts, and articles were unveiled that made reference to the life and accomplishments of a special man who is not known by many scholars of the period.

The publication of Clarke's *Narrative* was the springboard that led him to become the confidant, friend, and political strategist of anti-slavery advocates such as Lewis Tappan, Frederick Douglass, Harriet Beecher Stowe, John Brown, Gerrit Smith, Congressman Cassius Marcellus Clay, Lydia Maria Child, Dr. Martin Delaney, William Storum, Henry Bibb, and William Lloyd Garrison, among others.

W. P. Fuller, a respected columnist for the *Detroit Free Press,* knew Clarke for more than thirty years and considered him a friend. Clarke talked with Fuller freely over that period of time. Fuller said that Clarke never displayed subservience to any man, noting that Clarke treated everybody with respect but called no man his master. Yet the story of his life is the story of kindness and self-sacrifice in behalf of the colored race.[53]

Fuller wrote a commemorative article about the career of Clarke after his death in December of 1897 at the age of eighty-two.[54] Fuller concluded with a reference to the celebration of the emancipation of slaves after the end of the Civil War:

> With the magnates of the day of celebration, black and white, rode a man who saw in this event the consummation of a work to which he had devoted the greater portion of his life; a man who appreciated and understood the responsibility and importance which it brought to the colored race, better perhaps than any of them all, and that man was Lewis Clarke, the George Harris of *Uncle Tom's Cabin.*

The article was telegraphed throughout the world.

From a close reading of *The Narrative of the Sufferings of Lewis Clarke,* I am sure that Clarke would have added to Fuller's tribute that the emancipation was of importance to all citizens of the United States. I hope this brief introduction will allow more Americans to become better acquainted with this remarkable figure in our national history.

NOTES

1   Tyrone Beason, "We Have a Unique Story to Tell," *Seattle Times*, January 16, 2005.

2   "Once a Famous Slave," *Washington Post*, May 12, 1890.

3   Ibid.

4   See historian John Hope Franklin's *From Slavery to Freedom* (New York: Knopf, 1956): "The most distinguished honor that Bannaker received was his appointment to serve on the commission to define the boundary-line and lay out the streets in the District of Columbia" (136). Bannaker' name was submitted to President Washington by Thomas Jefferson.

5   Lewis and Milton Clarke, *Narratives of the Sufferings of Lewis and Milton Clarke: Sons of a Soldier of the Revolution During Captivity of More than Twenty-Five Years Among the Slaveholders of Kentucky, One of the So Called Christian States of North America* (Boston: Bela Marsh, 1846), 8.

6   John Gwathmey, *Historical Register of Virginians in the Revolution 1775–1783*. Quintin Publications Collection, Genealogical Publishing Company, Inc., 1979.

7   Young E. Allison, "Uncle Tom's Cabin," *Louisville Courier*, May 16, 1881, 3.

8   Lewis and Milton Clarke, *Narratives of the Sufferings of Lewis and Milton Clarke*, 8

9   Ibid.

10 "She was 'Little Eva,'" *Boston Daily Globe*, November 11, 1894, 29.

11 Ibid.

12 Lewis Clarke, *Narrative of the Sufferings of Lewis Clarke: During Captivity of More than Twenty-Five Years, Among the Algerines of Kentucky, One of the So Called Christian States of North America* (Boston: David H. Ela, 1845), 9.

13 Massachusetts Revolutionary War Records, vol. 3, p. 591. Secretary of the Commonwealth. Boston MA: Wright and Potter Printing, 1896–1908.

14 Clarke, *Narrative of the Sufferings of Lewis Clarke*, 9.

15 Jean Vacheenas and Betty Volk, "Born in Bondage: History of a Slave Family," *Negro History Bulletin*, May, 1973.

16 Lewis and Milton Clarke, *Narratives of the Sufferings of Lewis and Milton Clarke*, 8–11.

17 Ibid., 112, 113.

18 Ibid., 122.

19 Lydia Maria Child, "Leaves from a Slave's Journal of Life," *New York Anti-Slavery Standard*, October 20 and 27, 1842.

20 Harriet Beecher Stowe, *Key to Uncle Tom's Cabin: The Original Facts and Documents Upon Which the Story Is Founded, Together with Corroborative Statements Verifying the Truth of the Work* (London: Thomas Bosworth, 1853), 29.

21 Lewis and Milton Clarke, *Narratives of the Sufferings of Lewis and Milton Clarke,* 118–19.

22 "Lewis George Clarke, the Prototype of a Character in 'Uncle Tom's Cabin,'" *Stevens Point (WI) Journal,* August 21, 1896.

23 Clarke, *Narrative of the Sufferings of Lewis Clarke,* 1.

24 Allison, "Uncle Tom's Cabin", 1.

25 Clarke, *Narrative of the Sufferings of Lewis Clarke,* 24.

26 Ibid.

27 Ibid., 28.

28 James Allison, "The Historical Background of Harriett Beecher Stowe's Uncle Tom's Cabin," *Evansville (IN) Journal,* April, 15, 1881.

29 Ibid.

30 Ibid.

31 "Lewis George Clarke."

32 Ibid.

33 "'Uncle Tom's Cabin': An Interview with Lewis Clark, the 'George Harris' of the Story," *Chicago Tribune,* August 30, 1880.

34 Clarke, *Narrative of the Sufferings of Lewis Clarke,* 31–35.

35 Ibid., 38–39.

36 Ibid., 44–45.

37 Ibid., 55.

38 Franklin, "Captors Caught," *The Philanthropist,* October 22, 1842.

39 Y. E. Allison, "Uncle Tom's Cabin," 4.

40 Samuel Morison, Henry Commager, and William Leuchtenburg, *The Growth of the American Republic* (New York: Oxford University Press, 1980), 501–3.

41 Child, "Leaves from a Slave's Journal of Life."

42 John W. Blassingame, "Introduction," in Frederick Douglass, *Narrative of the Life of Frederick Douglass: An American Slave,* ed. John W. Blassingame, John R. McKivigan, and Peter P. Hinks (New Haven: Yale University Press, 2001), xvi.

43 "Uncle Tom's Cabin," *The Chicago Tribune*

44 Stowe, *Key to Uncle Tom's Cabin,* 18–19.

45 Y. E. Allison, "Uncle Tom's Cabin," 4.

46 Ibid.

47   "Once a Famous Slave."

48   Y. E. Allison, "Uncle Tom's Cabin," 6.

49   "Not Uncle Tom," *Evening Bulletin* (Maysville, KY), December 9, 1895.

50   Key to Uncle Tom's Cabin, p. 29.

51   Robert Teamoh, "The Half Not Told," *Boston Globe,* May 20, 1891.

52   Joan Hedrick, in *Harriet Beecher Stowe: A Life,* points out that the tour of
     Great Britain garnered more than triple the sales in the United States, reach-
     ing a million and a half the first year—1853.

53   "A Figure in History, *Detroit Free Press,* February, 19, 1898.

54   Ibid.

Lewis Clarke

NARRATIVE

OF THE

SUFFERINGS OF LEWIS CLARKE,

DURING A

CAPTIVITY

OF MORE THAN TWENTY-FIVE YEARS,

AMONG THE

ALGERINES OF KENTUCKY,

ONE OF THE SO CALLED

CHRISTIAN STATES OF NORTH AMERICA.

DICTATED BY HIMSELF.

BOSTON:

DAVID H. ELA, PRINTER,
AT THE STONE STEPS, 37 CORNHILL.

1845.

PREFACE.

I FIRST became acquainted with LEWIS CLARKE in December, 1842. I well remember the deep impression made upon my mind on hearing his Narrative from his own lips. It gave me a new and more vivid impression of the wrongs of Slavery than I had ever before felt. Evidently a person of good native talents and of deep sensibilities, such a mind had been under the dark cloud of slavery for more than twenty-five years. Letters, reading, all the modes of thought awakened by them, had been utterly hid from his eyes ; and yet his mind had evidently been active, and trains of thought were flowing through it, which he was utterly unable to express. I well remember too the wave on wave of deep feeling excited in an audience of more than a thousand persons, at Hallowell, Me., as they listened to his story and looked upon his energetic and manly countenance, and wondered if the dark cloud of slavery could cover up — hide from the world, and degrade to the condition of brutes, *such* immortal minds. His story, there and wherever since told, has aroused the most utter abhorrence of the Slave System.

For the two last years, I have had the most ample opportunity of becoming acquainted with Mr. Clarke. He has made this place his home, when not engaged in giving to public audiences the story of his sufferings, and the sufferings of his fellow slaves. Soon after he came to Ohio, by the faithful instruction of pious friends, he was led, as he believes, to see himself a sinner before God, and to seek pardon and forgiveness through the precious blood of the Lamb. He has ever manifested an ardent thirst for religious, as well as for other kinds of knowledge. In the opinion of all those best acquainted with him, he has maintained the character of a sincere Christian. That he is what he professes to be, — a slave escaped from the grasp of avarice and power, — there is not the least shadow of doubt. His narrative bears the most conclusive internal evidence of its truth. Persons of discriminating minds have heard it repeatedly, under a great variety of circumstances, and the story, in all substantial respects, has been always the same. He has been repeatedly recognized in the Free States by persons who knew him in Kentucky, when a slave. During the summer of 1844, Cassius M. Clay visited Boston, and on seeing Milton Clarke, recognized him as one of the Clarke family, well known to him in Kentucky. Indeed, nothing can be more surely established than the fact that Lewis and Milton Clarke are no impostors. For three years they have been engaged in telling their story in seven or eight different States, and no one has appeared to make an attempt to contradict them. The capture of Milton in Ohio, by the kidnappers, as a *slave*, makes assurance doubly strong. Wherever they have told their story, large audiences have collected, and every-

where they have been listened to with great interest and satisfaction.

Cyrus is fully equal to either of the brothers in sprightliness of
mind — is withal a great wit, and would make an admirable lec-
turer, but for an unfortunate impediment in his speech. They
all feel deeply the wrongs they have suffered, and are by no
means forgetful of their brethren in *bonds.* When Lewis first
came to this place, he was frequently noticed in silent and deep
meditation. On being asked what he was thinking of, he would
reply, " O, of the poor slaves ! Here I am free, and they suffering *so much.*" Bitter tears are often seen coursing down his
manly cheeks, as he recurs to the scenes of his early suffering.
Many persons, who have heard him lecture, have expressed a
strong desire that his story might be recorded in a connected
form. He has therefore concluded to have it printed. He was
anxious to add facts from other witnesses, and some appeals
from other hearts, if by any means he might awaken more hearts
to feel for his downtrodden brethren. Nothing seems to grieve
him to the heart like finding a minister of the Gospel, or a pro-
fessed Christian, indifferent to the condition of the slave. As to
doing much for the instruction of the minds of the slaves, or for
the salvation of their souls, till they are EMANCIPATED, *restored*
to the rights of men, in his opinion it is utterly impossible.

When the master, or his representative, the man who justifies
slaveholding, comes with the whip in one hand and the Bible in
the other, the slave says, at least in his heart, lay down *one* or
the *other.* Either make the tree good and the fruit good, or
else both corrupt together. Slaves do not believe that THE RE-

LIGION which is from God, bears *whips and chains.* They ask
emphatically concerning their FATHER in Heaven,

> " Has HE bid you buy and sell us,
> Speaking from his throne, the sky."

For the facts contained in the following Narrative, Mr. Clarke
is of course alone responsible. Yet having had the most ample
opportunities for testing his accuracy, I do not hesitate to say,
that I have not a shadow of doubt, but in all material points every
word is true. Much of it is in his own language, and all of it
according to his own dictation.

J. C. LOVEJOY.

Cambridgeport, April, 1845.

NARRATIVE OF LEWIS CLARKE.

I was born in March, as near as I can ascertain, in the year 1815, in Madison County, Kentucky, about seven miles from Richmond, upon the plantation of my grandfather, Samuel Campbell. He was considered a very respectable man among his fellow robbers — the slaveholders. It did not render him less honorable in their eyes, that he took to his bed Mary, his slave, perhaps half white, by whom he had one daughter, — LETITIA CAMPBELL. This was before his marriage.

My Father was from "beyond the flood"— from Scotland, and by trade a weaver. He had been married in his own country, and lost his wife, who left to him, as I have been told, two sons. He came to this country in time to be in the earliest scenes of the American Revolution. He was at the Battle of Bunker Hill, and continued in the army to the close of the war. About the year 1800, or before, he came to Kentucky, and married Miss Letitia Campbell, then held as a slave by her *dear* and *affectionate* father. My father died, as near as I can recollect, when I was about ten or twelve years of age. He had received a wound in the war which made him lame as long as he lived. I have often heard him tell of Scotland, sing the merry songs of his native land, and long to see its hills once more.

Mr. Campbell promised my father that his daughter Letitia should be made free in his will. It was with this promise that he married her. And I have no doubt that Mr. Campbell was as good as his word, and that by his *will*, my mother and her nine children were made free. But ten persons in one family, each worth three hundred dollars, are not easily set free among those accustomed to live by continued robbery. We did not, therefore, by an instrument from the hand of the dead, escape the avaricious grab of the slaveholder. It is the common belief that the will was destroyed by the heirs of Mr. Campbell.

The night in which I was born, I have been told, was dark and terrible, black as the night for which Job prayed, when he besought the clouds to pitch their tent round about the place of his birth ; and my life of slavery was but too exactly prefigured by the stormy elements that hovered over the first hour of my being. It was with great difficulty that any one could be urged out for a necessary attendant for my mother. At length one of the sons of Mr. Campbell, William, by the promise from his mother of the child that should be born, was induced to make an effort to obtain the necessary assistance. By going five or six miles he obtained a female professor of the couch.

William Campbell, by virtue of this title, always claimed me as his property. And well would it have been for me, if this claim had been regarded. At the age of six or seven years I fell into the hands of his sister, Mrs. Betsey Banton, whose character will be best known

when I have told the horrid wrongs which she heaped
upon me for ten years. If there are any *she* spirits that
come up from hell, and take possession of one part of
mankind, I am sure she is one of that sort. I was con-
signed to her under the following circumstances: When
she was married, there was given her, as part of her
dower, as is common among the Algerines of Kentucky,
a *girl* by the name of Ruth, about fourteen or fifteen
years old. In a short time Ruth was dejected and injured,
by beating and abuse of different kinds, so that she was
sold for a half-fool to the more tender mercies of the sugar
planter in Louisiana. The amiable Mrs. Betsey obtained
then, on loan from her parents, another slave named
Phillis. In six months she had suffered so severely under
the hand of this monster woman, that she made an attempt to kill herself, and was taken home by the parents of
Mrs. Banton. This produced a regular slave-holding family
brawl — a regular war of *four* years, between the *mild*
and peaceable Mrs. B. and her own parents. These wars
are very common among the Algerines in Kentucky; indeed, slave-holders have not arrived at that degree of civilization that enables them to live in tolerable peace, though
united by the nearest family ties. In them is fulfilled
what I have heard read in the Bible: The father is
against the son, and the daughter-in-law against the
mother-in-law, and their *foes* are of their own household.
Some of the slaveholders may have a *wide* house; but
one of the *cat-handed*, snake-eyed, brawling women,
which slavery produces, can fill it from cellar to garret. I
have heard every place I could get into any way, ring with
their screech-owl voices. Of all the animals on the face
of this earth, I am most afraid of a real mad, passionate,

raving, slaveholding woman. Some body told me once, that Edmund Burke declared, that the natives of India fled to the jungles, among tigers and lions, to escape the more barbarous cruelty of Warren Hastings. I am sure I would sooner lie down to sleep by the side of tigers. than near a raging-mad slave woman. But I must go back to *sweet* Mrs. Banton. I have been describing her in the *abstract* ; — I will give a full-grown portrait of her, right away. For four years after the trouble about Phillis, she never came near her father's house. At the end of this period another of the amiable sisters was to be married, and sister Betsey could not repress the tide of curiosity, urging her to be present at the nuptial ceremonies. Beside, she had another motive. Either shrewdly suspecting that she might deserve less than any member of the family, or that some ungrounded partiality would be manifested toward her sister, she determined at all hazards to be present, and see that the scales which weighed out the children of the plantation should be held with even hand. The wedding day was appointed — the sons and daughters of this joyful occasion were gathered together, and then came also the fair-faced, but black-hearted Mrs. B. Satan among the sons of God was never less welcome, than this fury among her kindred. They all knew what she came for, — to make mischief if possible. " Well now, if there aint Bets," exclaimed the old lady. The father was moody and silent, knowing that she inherited largely of the disposition of her mother; but he had experienced too many of her retorts of courtesy to say as much, for dear experience had taught him the discretion of silence. The brothers smiled at the prospect of fun and frolick, the sisters trembled for fear, and word flew round among the slaves, "The old she-bear has come home! look out! look out!"

The wedding went forward. Polly, a very good sort of a girl to be raised in that region, was married, and received, as the first installment of her dower, a *girl* and a *boy*. Now was the time for Mrs. Banton, sweet good Mrs. Banton. "Poll has a girl and a *boy*, and I only had that fool of a girl; I reckon if I go home without a boy too, this house wont be left standing."

This was said, too, while the sugar of the wedding cake was yet melting upon her tongue; how the bitter words would flow when the guests had retired, all began to imagine. To arrest this whirlwind of rising passion, her mother promised any boy upon the plantation, to be taken home on her return. Now my evil star was right in the top of the sky. Every boy was ordered in, to pass before this female sorceress, that she might select a victim for her unprovoked malice, and on whom to pour the vials of her wrath for years. I was that unlucky fellow. Mr. Campbell, my grandfather, objected, because it would divide a family, and offered her Moses, whose father and mother had been sold South. Mrs. Campbell put in for William's claim, dated *ante-natum* — before I was born; but objections and claims of every kind were swept away by the wild passion and shrill-toned voice of Mrs. B. Me she would have, and none else. Mr. Campbell went out to hunt and drive away bad thoughts — the old lady became quiet, for she was sure none of her blood run in my veins, and if there was any of her husband's there, it was no fault of hers. I was too young, only seven years of age, to understand what was going on. But my poor and affectionate mother understood and appreciated it all. When

2

she left the kitchen of the Mansion House, where she was employed as cook, and came home to her own little cottage, the tear of anguish was in her eye, and the image of sorrow upon every feature of her face. She knew the female Nero, whose rod was now to be over me. That night sleep departed from her eyes; with the youngest child clasped firmly to her bosom, she spent the night in walking the floor, coming ever and anon to lift up the clothes and look at me and my poor brother who lay sleeping together. *Sleeping*, I said ; brother slept, but not I. I saw my mother when she first came to me; and I could not sleep. The vision of that night, its deep, ineffaceable impression is now before my mind with all the distinctness of yesterday. In the morning I was put into the carriage with Mrs. B. and her children, and my weary pilgrimage of suffering was fairly begun. It was her business on the road for about twenty five or thirty miles to initiate her children into the art of tormenting their new victim. I was seated upon the bottom of the carriage, and these little imps were employed in pinching me, pulling my ears and hair, and they were stirred up by their mother like a litter of young wolves to torment me in every way possible. In the mean time I was compelled by the old she wolf, to call them " Master," " Mistress," and bow to them and obey them at the first call.

During that day, I had indeed no very agreeable foreboding of the torments to come ; but sad as were my anticipations, the reality was infinitely beyond them. Infinitely more bitter than death were the cruelties I experienced at the hand of this merciless woman. Save from one or two slaves on the plantation, during my ten years of captivity here, I scarcely heard a kind word, or saw a smile

toward me from any living being. And now that I am
where people look kind and act kindly toward me, it
seems like a dream. I hardly seem to be in the same
world that I was then. When I first got into the free
States and saw every body look like they loved one
another, sure enough I thought this must be the *"Heaven"*
of LOVE I had heard something about. But I must go
back to what I suffered from that wicked woman. It is
hard work to keep the mind upon it; I hate to think it
over — but I must tell it — the world must know what is
done in Kentucky. I cannot, however, tell all the ways,
by which she tormented me, I can only give a few instances of my suffering as specimens of the whole. A book of
a thousand pages would not be large enough to tell of all
the tears I shed, and the sufferings endured in THAT TEN
YEARS OF PURGATORY.

A very trivial offence was sufficient to call forth a great
burst of indignation from this woman of ungoverned passions. In my simplicity, I put my lips to the same vessel
and drank out of it from which her children were accustomed to drink. She expressed her utter abhorrence of
such an act, by throwing my head violently back, and
dashing into my face two dippers of water. The shower
of water was followed by a heavier shower of *kicks* — yes,
delicate reader, this *lady* did not hesitate to *kick*, as well
as cuff in a very plentiful manner — but the words bitter
and cutting that followed were like a storm of hail upon
my young heart. " She would teach me better manners
than that — she would let me know I was to be brought up
to her hand — she would have *one* slave that knew his
place ; if I wanted water, go to the spring, and not drink
there in the house." This was new times for me — for

some days I was completely benumbed with my sorrow. I
could neither eat nor sleep.   If there is any human being
on earth, who has been so blessed as never to have *tasted*
the cup of sorrow, and therefore is unable to conceive of
suffering, if there be one so lost to all feeling as even to
say that the slaves do not suffer, when *families* are separated, let such an one go to the ragged quilt which was
my couch and pillow and stand there night after night, for
long weary hours, and see the bitter tears streaming down
the face of that more than orphan boy, while with half suppressed sighs and sobs, he calls again and again upon
his absent mother.

> " Say, Mother, wast thou conscious of the tears I shed, —
> Hovered thy spirit o'er thy sorrowing son ?
> Wretch even *then !* Life's journey just begun."

Let him stand by that couch of bitter sorrow through the
terribly lonely night, and then wring out the wet end of
those rags, and see how many tears yet remain, after the
burning temples had absorbed all they could.   He will not
doubt, he cannot doubt but the slave has feeling.   But I
find myself running away again from Mrs. Banton — and I
do n't much wonder neither.

There were several children in the family, and my first
main business was to wait upon them.   Another young
slave and myself have often been compelled to sit up by
turns all night, to rock the cradle of a little, peevish scion
of slavery.   If the cradle was stopped, the moment they
awoke a dolorous cry was sent forth to mother or father,
that Lewis had gone to sleep.   The reply to this call,
would be a direction from the mother, for these petty ty-
rants to get up and take the whip, and give the good-for-

nothing scoundrel a smart whipping. This was the mid-night pastime of a child ten or twelve years old. What might you expect of the future man?

There were four house-slaves in this family, including myself, and though we had not, in all respects, so hard work as the field hands, yet in many things our condition was much worse. We were constantly exposed to the whims and passions of every member of the family; from the least to the greatest their anger was wreaked upon us. Nor was our life an easy one, in the hours of our toil or in the amount of labor performed. We were always required to sit up until all the family had retired; then we must be up at early dawn in summer, and before day in winter. If we failed, through weariness or for any other reason, to appear at the first morning summons, we were sure to have our hearing quickened by a severe chastisement. Such horror has seized me, lest I might not hear the first shrill call, that I have often in dreams fancied I heard that un-welcome call, and have leaped from my couch and walked through the house and out of it before I awoke. I have gone and called the other slaves, in my sleep, and asked them if they did not hear master call. Never, while I live, will the remembrance of those long, bitter nights of fear pass from my mind.

But I want to give you a few specimens of the abuse which I received. During the ten years that I lived with Mrs. Banton, I do not think there were as many days, when she was at home, that I, or some other slave, did not re-ceive some kind of beating or abuse at her hands. It seemed as though she could not live nor sleep unless some poor back was smarting, some head beating with pain, or some eye filled with tears, around her. Her tender mer-

2*

cies were indeed cruel. She brought up her children to
imitate her example. Two of them manifested some dislike to the cruelties taught them by their mother, but they
never stood high in favor with her; indeed, any thing
like humanity or kindness to a slave, was looked upon by
her as a great offence.

Her instruments of torture were ordinarily the raw hide,
or a bunch of hickory-sprouts seasoned in the fire and tied
together. But if these were not at hand, nothing came
amiss. She could relish a beating with a chair, the broom,
tongs, shovel, shears, knife-handle, the heavy heel of her
slipper; her zeal was so active in these barbarous inflic-
tions, that her invention was wonderfully quick, and some
way of inflicting the requisite torture was soon found out.

One instrument of torture is worthy of particular description. *This was an oak club, a foot and a half in
length and an inch and a half square.* With this delicate weapon she would beat us upon the hands and upon
the feet until they were blistered. This instrument was
carefully preserved for a period of four years. Every day,
for that time, I was compelled to see that hated tool of
cruelty lying in the chair by my side. The least degree of
delinquency either in not doing all the appointed work, or
in look or behavior, was visited with a beating from this
oak club. That club will always be a prominent object in
the picture of horrors of my life of more than twenty years
of bitter bondage.

When about nine years old I was sent in the evening
to catch and kill a turkey. They were securely sleeping
in a tree — their accustomed resting place for the night.
I approached as cautiously as possible, selected the victim
I was directed to catch, but just as I grasped him in my

hand, my foot slipped and he made his escape from the tree and fled beyond my reach. I returned with a heavy heart to my mistress with the story of my misfortune. She was enraged beyond measure. She determined at once that I should have a whipping of the worst kind, and she was bent upon adding all the aggravations possible. Master had gone to bed drunk, and was now as fast asleep as drunkards ever are. At any rate he was filling the house with the noise of his snoring and with the perfume of his breath. I was ordered to go and call him — wake him up — and ask him to be *kind* enough to give me fifty good smart lashes. To be *whipped* is bad enough — to *ask* for it is worse — to ask a drunken man to whip you is too bad. I would sooner have gone to a nest of rattlesnakes, than to the bed of this drunkard. But go I must. Softly I crept along, and gently shaking his arm, said with a trembling voice, "Master, Master, Mistress wants you to wake up." This did not go the extent of her command, and in a great fury she called out — "What, you wont ask him to whip you, will you?" I then added "Mistress wants you to give me fifty lashes." A bear at the smell of a lamb, was never roused quicker. "Yes, yes, that I will; I'll give you such a whipping as you will never want again." And sure enough so he did. He sprang from the bed, seized me by the hair, lashed me with a handful of switches, threw me my whole length upon the floor, beat, kicked and cuffed me worse than he would a dog, and then threw me, with all his strength out of the door more dead than alive. There I lay for a long time scarcely able and not daring to move, till I could hear no sound of the furies within, and then crept to my couch, longing for death to put an end to my misery. I had no friend in the

world to whom I could utter one word of complaint, or to
whom I could look for protection.

Mr. Banton owned a blacksmith shop in which he spent
some of his time, though he was not a very efficient hand
at the forge.   One day Mistress told me to go over to the
shop and let Master give me a flogging.   I knew the mode
of punishing there too well. I would rather die than go. The
poor fellow who worked in the shop, a very skilful workman,
neglected one day to pay over a half dollar that he had received of a customer for a job of work.   This was quite an
unpardonable offence.   No right is more strictly maintained by slave holders, than the right they have to every cent
of the slave's wages.   The slave kept fifty cents of his own
wages in his pocket one night.   This came to the knowledge
of the Master.   He called for the money and it was not
spent — it was handed to him; but there was the horrid *intention* of keeping it.   The enraged Master put a handful
of nail rods into the fire, and when they were *red hot* took
them out, and *cooled* one after another of them in the
blood and flesh of the poor slave's back.   I knew this was
the shop mode of punishment; I would not go, and Mr.
Banton came home, and his amiable lady told him the
story of my refusal ; he broke forth in a great rage, and
gave me a most unmerciful beating, adding that if I had
come, he would have burned the hot nail rods into my back.

Mrs. Banton, as is common among slave holding women,
seemed to hate and abuse me all the more, because I had
some of the blood of her father in my veins.   There is no
slaves that are so badly abused, as those that are related to
some of the women — or the children of their own husband ; it seems as though they never could hate these quite
bad enough.   My sisters were as white and good look-

ing as any of the young ladies in Kentucky. It happened once of a time, that a young man called at the house of Mr. Campbell, to see a sister of Mrs. Banton. Seeing one of my sisters in the house and pretty well dressed, with a strong family look, he thought it was Miss Campbell, and with that supposition addressed some conversation to her which he had intended for the private ear of Miss C. The mistake was noised abroad and occasioned some amusement to young people. Mrs. Banton heard, it made her cauldron of wrath sizzling hot — every thing that diverted and amused other people seemed to enrage her. There are hot springs in Kentucky, she was just like one of them, only chuckfull of boiling poison.

She must wreak her vengeance for this innocent mistake of the young man, upon me. "She would fix me so that nobody should ever think I was white." Accordingly in a burning hot day, she *made me take off every rag of clothes, go out into the garden* and pick herbs for hours — in order to *burn* me black. When I went out she threw cold water on me so that the sun might take effect upon me, when I came in she gave me a severe beating on my blistered back.

After I had lived with Mrs. B. three or four years I was put to spinning hemp, flax and tow, on an old fashioned foot wheel. There were four or five slaves at this business a good part of the time. We were kept at our work from daylight to dark in summer, from long before day to nine or ten o'clock in the evening in winter. Mrs. Banton for the most part was near or kept continually passing in and out to see that each of us performed as much work as she thought we ought to do. Being young and sick at heart all the time, it was very hard work to go

through the day and evening and not suffer exceedingly
for want of more sleep. Very often too I was compelled
to work beyond the ordinary hour to finish the appointed
task of the day. Sometimes I found it impossible not to
drop asleep at the wheel.

On these occasions Mrs. B. had her peculiar contrivan-
ces for keeping us awake. She would sometimes sit by
the hour with a dipper of vinegar and salt, and throw it in
my eyes to keep them open. My hair was pulled till
there was no longer any pain from that source. *And I
can now suffer myself to be lifted by the hair of the head,
without experiencing the least pain.*

She very often kept me from getting water to satisfy my
thirst, and in one instance kept me for two entire days
without a particle of food.

But all my severe labor, bitter and cruel punishments for
these ten years of captivity with this worse than Arab family, all these were as nothing to the sufferings experienced
by being separated from my mother, brothers and sisters ;
the same things, with them near to sympathize with me, to
hear my story of sorrow, would have been comparatively
tolerable.

They were distant only about thirty miles, and yet in
ten long, lonely years of childhood, I was only permitted to
see them three times.

My mother occasionally found an opportunity to send
me some token of remembrance and affection, a sugar
plum or an apple, but I scarcely ever ate them — they were
laid up and handled and wept over till they wasted away
in my hand.

My thoughts continually by day and my dreams by
night were of mother and home, and the horror experi-

enced in the morning, when I awoke and behold it was
a dream, is beyond the power of language to describe.

But I am about to leave the den of robbers where I had
been so long imprisoned. I cannot however call the reader from his new and pleasant acquaintance with this
amiable pair, without giving a few more incidents of their
history. When this is done, and I have taken great pains,
as I shall do to put a copy of this portrait in the hands of
this Mrs. B., I shall bid her farewell. If she sees something awfully hideous in her picture as here presented, she
will be constrained to acknowledge it is true to nature — I
have given it from no malice, no feeling of resentment toward her, but that the world may know what is done by
slavery, and that slave holders may know, that their crimes
will come to light. I hope and pray that Mrs. B. will repent
of her many and aggravated sins before it is too late.

The scenes between her and her husband while I was with
them strongly illustrate the remark of Jefferson, that slavery
fosters the worst passions of the master. Scarcely a day
passed in which bitter words were not bandied from one to
the other. I have seen Mrs. B. with a large knife drawn
in her right hand, the other upon the collar of her husband,
swearing and threatening to cut him *square in two.*
They both drank freely, and swore like highwaymen. He
was a gambler and a counterfeiter. I have seen and handled his moulds and his false coin. They finally quarrelled
openly and separated, and the last I knew of them, he was
living a sort of poor vagabond life in his native State,
and she was engaged in a protracted law suit with some
of her former friends about her father's property.

Of course such habits did not produce great thrift in
their worldly condition, and myself and other slaves were

mortgaged from time to time to make up the deficiency between their income and expenses. I was transferred at the
age of sixteen or seventeen to a Mr. K., whose name I forbear to mention, lest if he or any other man should ever
claim *property* where they never had any, this my own
testimony might be brought in to aid their wicked purposes.

In the exchange of masters, my condition was in many
respects greatly improved — I was free at any rate from
that kind of suffering experienced at the hand of Mrs. B.
as though she delighted in cruelty for its own sake. My
situation however with Mr. K. was far from enviable.
Taken from the work in and around the house, and put
at once at that early age to the constant work of a full
grown man, I found it not an easy task always to escape
the lash of the overseer. In the four or five years that I
was with this man, the overseers were often changed.
Sometimes we had a man that seemed to have some consideration, some mercy, but generally their eye seemed to
be fixed upon one object, and that was to get the greatest
possible amount of work out of every slave upon the plantation. When stooping to clear the tobacco plants from
the worms which infest them, a work which draws most
cruelly upon the back, some of these men would not
allow us a moment to rest at the end of the row, but at
the crack of the whip we were compelled to jump to our
places from row to row for hours; while the poor back
was crying out with torture. Any complaint or remon-
stance under such circumstances is sure to be answered in
no other way than by the lash. As a sheep before her
shearers is dumb, so a slave is not permitted to open his
mouth.

There were about one hundred and fifty slaves upon

this plantation. Generally we had enough in quantity of food. We had however but two meals a day, of corn meal bread, and soup, or meat of the poorest kind. Very often so little care had been taken to cure and preserve the bacon, that when it came to us, though it had been fairly killed once, it was more alive than dead. Occasionally we had some refreshment over and above the two meals, but this was extra, beyond the rules of the plantation. And to balance this gratuity, we were also frequently deprived of our food as a punishment. We suffered greatly, too, for want of water. The slave drivers have the notion that slaves are more healthy if allowed to drink but little, than they are if freely allowed nature's beverage. The slaves quite as confidently cherish the opinion, that if the master would drink less peach brandy and whisky, and give the slave more water, it would be better all round. As it is, the more the master and overseer drink, the less they seem to think the slave needs.

In the winter we took our meals before day in the morning and after work at night. In the summer at about nine o'clock in the morning and at two in the afternoon. When we were cheated out of our two meals a day, either by the cruelty or caprice of the overseer, we always felt it a kind of special duty and privilege to make up in some way the deficiency. To accomplish this we had many devices. And we sometimes resorted to our peculiar methods, when incited only by a desire to taste greater variety than our ordinary bill of fare afforded.

This sometimes lead to very disastrous results. The poor slave, who was caught with a chicken or a pig killed from the plantation, had his back scored most unmercifully. Nevertheless, the pigs would die without being sick or

3

squealing once, and the hens, chickens and turkeys, sometimes disappeared and never stuck up a feather to tell
where they were buried.   The old goose would sometimes
exchange her whole nest of eggs for round pebbles ; and
patient as that animal is, this quality was exhausted, and
she was obliged to leave her nest with no train of offspring
behind her.

One old slave woman upon this plantation was altogether
too keen and shrewd for the best of them.   She would go
out to the corn crib, with her basket, watch her opportunity, with one effective blow pop over a little pig, slip him
into her basket and put the cobs on top, trudge off to her
cabin, and look just as innocent as though she had a right
to eat of the work of her own hands.   It was a kind of first
principle, too, in her code of morals, that they that *worked*
had a right to eat.   The moral of all questions in relation
to taking food was easily settled by Aunt Peggy.   The
only question with her was, *how* and *when* to do it.

It could not be done openly, that was plain ; it must be
done, secretly, if not in the day time by all means in the
night.   With a dead pig in the cabin, and the water all
hot for scalding, she was at one time warned by her son
that the Philistines were upon her.   Her resources were
fully equally to the sudden emergency, quick as thought,
the pig was thrown into the boiling kettle, a door was put
over it, her daughter seated upon it, and with a good
thick quilt around her, the overseer found little Phillis taking a steam bath for a terrible cold.   The daughter acted
well her part, groaned sadly, the mother was very busy in
tucking in the quilt, and the overseer was blinded, and
went away without seeing a bristle of the pig.

Aunt P. cooked for herself, for another slave named

George, and for me. George was very successful in bringing home his share of the plunder. He could capture a pig or a turkey without exciting the least suspicion. The old lady often rallied me for want of courage for such enterprizes. At length, I summoned resolution one rainy night, and determined there should be one from the herd of swine brought home by my hands. I went to the crib of corn, got my ear to shell, and my cart stake to despatch a little roaster. I raised my arm to strike, summoned courage again and again, but to no purpose. The scattered kernels were all picked up and no blow struck. Again I visited the crib, selected my victim, and *struck* — the blow glanced upon the side of the head, and instead of falling, he ran off squealing louder than ever I heard a pig squeal before. I ran as fast in an opposite direction, made a large circuit and reached the cabin — emptied the hot water and made for my couch as soon as possible. I escaped detection, and only suffered from the ridicule of old Peggy and young George.

Poor Jess, upon the same plantation, did not so easily escape. More successful in his effort, he killed his pig, but he was found out. He was hung up by the hands, with a rail between his feet, and full three hundred lashes scored in upon his naked back. For a long time his life hung in doubt, and his poor wife, for becoming a partaker after the fact, was most severely beaten.

Another slave, employed as a driver upon the plantation, was compelled to whip his own wife, for a similar offence, so severely that she never recovered from the cruelty. She was literally *whipped to death by her own husband.*

A slave, called Hall, the hostler on the plantation, made a successful sally one night upon the animals forbidden to

the Jews. The next day he went into the barn loft and
fell asleep. While sleeping over his abundant supper.
and dreaming perhaps of his feast, he heard the shrill voice
of his master, crying out " the hogs are at the horse trough
— where is Hall." The " hogs and Hall " coupled together, were enough for the poor fellow. He sprung from
the hay and made the best of his way off the plantation.
He was gone six months, and at the end of this period he
procured the intercession of the son-in-law of his master,
and returned, escaping the ordinary punishment. But the
transgression was laid up. Slave holders seldom *forgive*,
they only *postpone* the time of revenge. When about to
be severely flogged for some pretended offence, he took
two of his grandsons and escaped as far towards Canada
as Indiana. He was followed, captured, brought back
and whipped most horribly. All the old score had been
treasured up against him, and his poor back atoned for
the whole at once.

On this plantation was a slave named Sam, whose wife
lived a few miles distant, and Sam was very seldom permitted to go and see his family. He worked in the blacksmith shop. For a small offence, he was hung up by the
hands, a rail between his feet, and whipped in turn by the
master, overseer and one of the waiters, till his back was
torn all to pieces, and in less than two months Sam was
in his grave. His last words were, " Mother, tell master
he has killed me at last for nothing, but tell him if God
will forgive him, I will."

A very poor white woman lived within about a mile of
the plantation house. A female slave named Flora, knowing she was in a very suffering condition, shelled out a
peck of corn and carried it to her in the night. Next day

the old man found it out, and this deed of charity was atoned for by one hundred and fifty lashes upon the bare back of poor Flora.

The master with whom I now lived, was a very passionate man. At one time he thought the work on the plantation did not go on as it ought. One morning, when he and the overseer waked up from a drunken frolick, they swore the hands should not eat a morsel of any thing, till a field of wheat of some sixty acres was all cradled. There were from thirty to forty hands to do the work. We were driven on to the extent of our strength, and although a brook ran through the field, not one of us was permitted to stop and taste a drop of water. Some of the men were so exhausted, that they reeled for very weakness; two of the women fainted, and one of them was severely whipped to revive her. They were at last carried helpless from the field and thrown down under the shade of a tree. At about five o'clock in the afternoon the wheat was all cut and we were permitted to eat. Our suffering for want of water was excruciating. I trembled all over from the inward gnawing of hunger and from burning thirst.

In view of the sufferings of this day we felt fully justified in making a foraging expedition upon the milk room that night. And when master and overseer and all hands were locked up in sleep, ten or twelve of us went down to the spring house,—a house built over a spring to keep the milk and other things cool. We pressed altogether against the door, and open it came. We found half of a good baked pig, plenty of cream, milk and other delicacies, and as we felt in some measure delegated to represent all that had been cheated of their meals the day before, we ate plentifully. But after a successful plundering expedition

3*

within the gates of the enemy's camp, it is not easy always to cover the retreat. We had a *reserve* in the pasture for this purpose. We went up to the herd of swine, and with a milk pail in hand, it was easy to persuade them there was more where that came from, and the whole tribe followed readily into the spring house, and we left them there to wash the dishes and wipe up the floor, while we retired to rest. This was not malice in us; we did not love the waste which the hogs made; but we must have something to eat, to pay for the cruel and reluctant fast; and when we had obtained this, we must of course cover up our track. They watch us narrowly; and to take an egg, a pound of meat, or anything else, however hungry we may be, is considered a great crime, — we are compelled therefore, to waste a good deal sometimes, to get a little.

I lived with this Mr. K. about four or five years. I then fell into the hands of his son. He was a drinking, ignorant man, but not so cruel as his father. Of him I hired my time at $12 a month, boarded and clothed myself. To meet my payments, I split rails, burned coal, peddled grass seed, and took hold of whatever I could find to do. This last master, or owner as he would call himself, died about one year before I left Kentucky. By the administrators I was hired out for a time, and at last put up upon the auction block for sale. No *bid* could be obtained for me. There were two reasons in the way. One was, there were two or three old mortgages which were not settled, and the second reason given by the bidders was, I had had too many privileges — had been permitted to trade for myself and go over the state — in short, to use their phrase, I was a "spoilt nigger." And sure enough I was, for all their purposes. I had long thought and dreamed of LIBERTY; I was now determined to make an effort to gain it. No tongue can tell the doubt, the perplexities, the anxiety which a slave feels, when making up his mind upon this subject. If he makes an effort and is not successful, he must be laughed at by his fellows ; he will be beaten unmercifully by the master, and then watched and used the harder for it all his life.

And then if he gets away, *who, what* will he find ? He is ignorant of the world. All the white part of mankind, that he has ever seen, are enemies to him and all his kindred. How can he venture where none but white faces shall greet him ? The master tells him that abolitionists *decoy* slaves off into the free states to catch them and sell them to Louisiana or Mississippi ; and if he goes to Canada, the British will put him in a *mine under ground, with both eyes put out, for life.* How does he know what or whom to believe ? A horror of great darkness comes upon him, as he thinks over what may befal him. Long, very long time did I think of escaping before I made the effort.

At length the report was started that I was to be sold for Louisiana. Then I thought it was time to act. My mind was made up. This was about two weeks before I started. The first plan was formed between a slave named Isaac and myself. Isaac proposed to take one of the horses of his mistress, and I was to take my pony, and we were to ride off together, I as master and he as slave. We started together and went on five miles. My want of confidence in the plan induced me to turn back. Poor Isaac plead like a good fellow to go forward. I am satisfied from experience and observation that both of us must have been captured and carried back. I did not know enough at that time to travel and manage a waiter. Every thing

would have been done in such an awkward manner that a
keen eye would have seen through our plot at once.   I
did not know the roads, and could not have read the guide
boards ; and ignorant as many people are in Kentucky, they
would have thought it strange to see a man with a waiter,
who could not read a guide board.   I was sorry to leave
Isaac, but I am satisfied I could have done him no good in
the way proposed.

After this failure I staid about two weeks, and, after
having arranged every thing to the best of my knowledge,
I saddled my pony, went into the cellar where I kept my
grass seed apparatus, put my clothes into a pair of saddle-
bags, and them into my seed-bag, and thus equipped set
sail for the North Star.   O what a day was that to me.
This was on Saturday, in August, 1841.   I wore my common clothes, and was very careful to avoid special suspicion, as I already imagined the administrator was very
watchful of me.   The place from which I started was
about fifty miles from Lexington.   The reason why I do
not give the *name* of the place, and a more accurate location, must be obvious to any one who remembers that
in the eye of the law I am yet accounted a slave, and no
spot in the United States affords an asylum for the wan-
derer.   True, I feel protected in the hearts of the many
warm friends of the slave by whom I am surrounded, but
this protection does not come from the LAWS of any one of
the United States.

But to return.   After riding about fifteen miles, a Baptist minister overtook me on the road, saying, " How do
you do, boy ; are you free ?   I always thought you were free,
till I saw them try to sell you the other day."   I then
wished him a thousand miles off, preaching, if he would,

to the whole plantation, " Servants obey your masters ; "
but I wanted neither sermons, questions, nor advice from
him. At length I mustered resolution to make some kind
of a reply.—What made you think I was free? He replied, that he had noticed I had great privileges, that I did
much as I liked, and that I was almost white. O yes, I
said, but there are a great many slaves as white as I am.
" Yes," he said, and then went on to name several ; among
others, one who had lately, as he said, run away. This
was touching altogether too near upon what I was thinking of. Now, said I, he must know, or at least reckons,
what I am at — *running away*.

However, I blushed as little as possible, and made
strange of the fellow who had lately run away, as though
I knew nothing of it. The old fellow looked at me, as it
seemed to me, as though he would read my thoughts. I
wondered what in the world a *slave could* run away for,
especially if they had such a chance as I had had for the
last few years. He said, " I suppose you would not run
away on any account, you are so well treated." O, said
I, I do very well — very well, sir. If you should ever
hear that I had run away, be certain it must be because
there is some great change in my treatment.

He then began to talk with me about the seed in my
bag, and said that he should want to buy some. Then, I
thought, he means to get at the truth by looking in my
seed-bag, where, sure enough, he would not find *grass*
seed, but the seeds of Liberty. However, he dodged off
soon, and left me alone. And although I have heard say,
poor company is better than none, I felt much better without him than with him.

When I had gone on about twenty-five miles, I went

down into a deep valley by the side of the road, and changed my clothes. I reached Lexington about seven o'clock that evening, and put up with brother Cyrus. As I had often been to Lexington before, and stopped with him, it excited no attention from the slave holding gentry. Moreover, I had a pass from the administrator, of whom I had hired my time. I remained over the Sabbath with Cyrus, and we talked over a great many plans for future operations, if my efforts to escape should be successful. Indeed we talked over all sorts of ways for me to proceed. But both of us were very ignorant of the roads, and of the best way to escape suspicion. And I sometimes wonder, that a slave, so ignorant, so timid, as he is, *ever* makes the attempt to get his freedom. *" Without* are *foes, within* are *fears."*

Monday morning, bright and early, I set my face in good earnest toward the Ohio River, determined to see and tread the north bank of it, or *die* in the attempt. I said to myself, one of two things, FREEDOM or DEATH. The first night I reached Mayslick, fifty odd miles from Lexington. Just before reaching this village, I stopped to think over my situation, and determine how I would pass that night. On that night hung all my hopes. I was within twenty miles of Ohio. My horse was unable to reach the river that night. And besides, to travel and attempt to cross the river in the night, would excite suspicion. I must spend the night *there*. But *how?* At one time, I thought, I will take my pony out into the field and give him some corn, and sleep myself on the grass. But then the *dogs* will be out in the evening, and if caught under such circumstances, they will take me for a *thief* if not for a runaway. That will not do. So after weighing the matter all over, I made a plunge right into the heart of the village, and put up at the tavern.

After seeing my pony disposed of, I looked into the bar-room, and saw some persons that I thought were from my part of the country, and would know me. I shrunk back with horror. What to do I did not know. I looked across the street, and saw the shop of a silversmith. A thought of a pair of spectacles, to hide my face, struck me. I went across the way, and began to barter for a pair of double eyed green spectacles. When I got them on, they blind-folded *me*, if they did not others. Every thing seemed right up in my eyes. I hobbled back to the tavern, and called for supper. This I did to avoid notice, for I felt like any thing but eating. At tea I had not learned to measure distances with my new eyes, and the first pass I made with my knife and fork at my plate, went right into my cup. This confused me still more, and, after drinking one cup of tea, I left the table, and got off to bed as soon as possible. But not a wink of sleep that night. All was confusion, dreams, anxiety and trembling.

As soon as day dawned, I called for my horse, paid my reckoning, and was on my way, rejoicing that *that* night was gone, any how. I made all diligence on my way, and was across the Ohio, and in Aberdeen by noon that day !

What my feelings were when I reached the free shore, can be better imagined than described. I trembled all over with deep emotion, and I could feel my hair rise up on my head. I was on what was called a *free* soil, among a people who had no slaves. I saw white men at work, and no slave smarting beneath the lash. Every thing was indeed *new* and wonderful. Not knowing

where to find a friend, and being ignorant of the country,
— unwilling to inquire lest I should betray my ignorance,
it was a whole week before I reached Cincinnati. At one
place where I put up, I had a great many more questions
put to me than I wished to answer. At another place I
was very much annoyed by the officiousness of the landlord, who made it a point to supply every guest with news-
papers. I took the copy handed me, and turned it over
in a somewhat awkward manner, I suppose. He came to
me to point out a Veto, or some other very important
news. I thought it best to decline his assistance, and
gave up the paper, saying my eyes were not in a fit condition to read much.

At another place, the neighbors, on learning that a
Kentuckian was at the tavern, came in great earnestness
to find out what my business was. Kentuckians sometimes came there to kidnap their citizens — they were in
the habit of watching them close. I at length satisfied
them, by assuring them that I was not, nor my father before me, any slave holder at all; but, lest their suspicions
should be excited in another direction, I added, my grandfather was a slave holder.

At Cincinnati I found some old acquaintances, and spent
several days. In passing through some of the streets, I
several times saw a great slave dealer from Kentucky, who
knew me, and when I approached him, I was very careful
to give him a wide berth. The only advice that I here received, was from a man who had once been a slave. He
urged me to sell my pony, go up the river to Portsmouth,
then take the canal for Cleveland, and cross over to Canada. I acted upon this suggestion, sold my horse for a
small sum, as he was pretty well used up, took passage for

Portsmouth, and soon found myself on the canal-boat, headed for Cleveland. On the boat I became acquainted with a Mr. Conoly, from New York. He was very sick with fever and ague, and as he was a stranger and alone, I took the best possible care of him for a time. One day, in conversation with him, he spoke of the slaves in the most harsh and bitter language, and was especially severe on those who *attempted to run away.* Thinks I, you are not the man for me to have much to do with. I found the *spirit* of slaveholding was not all South of the Ohio River.

No sooner had I reached Cleveland, than a trouble came upon me from a very unexpected quarter. A rough, swearing, reckless creature in the shape of a man, came up to me and declared I had passed a bad five dollar bill upon his wife, in the boat, and he demanded the silver for it. I had never seen him nor his wife before. He pursued me into the tavern, swearing and threatening all the way. The travellers, that had just arrived at the tavern, were asked to give their names to the clerk, that he might enter them upon the book. He called on me for my name, just as this ruffian was in the midst of his assault upon me. On leaving Kentucky I thought it best for my own security to take a new name, and I had been entered on the boat, as Archibald Campbell. I knew, with such a charge as this man was making against me, it would not do to change my name from the boat to the hotel. At the moment, I could not recollect what I had called myself, and for a few minutes, I was in a complete puzzle. The clerk kept calling, and I made believe deaf, till at length the name popped back again, and I was duly enrolled a guest at the tavern in Cleveland. I had heard before of persons being frightened out of their *Christian* names, but I was fairly scared

4

out of both mine for a while.   The landlord soon protected
me from the violence of the bad-meaning man, and drove
him away from the house.

I was detained at Cleveland several days, not knowing
how to get across the Lake into Canada.   I went out to
the shore of the lake again and again, to try and see the
other side, but I could see no hill, mountain, nor city of the
asylum I sought.   I was afraid to inquire *where* it was, lest
it would betray such a degree of ignorance as to excite
suspicion at once.   One day I heard a man ask another,
employed on board a vessel, "and where does this vessel
trade?"   Well, I thought, if that is a proper question for
you, it is for me.   So I passed along and asked of every
vessel, " Where does this vessel trade?"   At last the
answer came, " over here in Kettle Creek, near Port Stanley."   And where is that, said I.   " O, right over here in
Canada."   That was the sound for me, " over here in Canada."   The captain asked me if I wanted a passage to Canada.   I thought it would not do to be too earnest about it,
lest it would betray me.   I told him I some thought of going,
if I could get a passage cheap.   We soon came to terms
on this point, and that evening we set sail.   After proceed-
ing only nine miles the wind changed, and the captain returned to port again.   This I thought was a very bad
omen.   However, I stuck by, and the next evening at nine
o'clock we set sail once more, and at daylight, we were in
Canada.

When I stepped ashore here, I said, sure enough I AM
FREE.   Good heaven! what a sensation, when it first visits
the bosom of a full grown man — one, *born* to bondage —
one, who had been taught from early infancy, that this was
his inevitable lot for life.   Not till *then*, did I dare to cherish

for a moment the feeling that *one* of the limbs of my body, was my own. The slaves often say, when cut in the hand or foot, "plague on the old foot, or the old hand, it is master's — let him take care of it — Nigger don't care if he never get well." My hands, my feet, were now my own. But what to do with them was the next question. A strange sky was over me, a new earth under me, strange voices all around — even the animals were such as I had never seen. A flock of prairie hens and some black geese, were entirely new to me. I was entirely alone, no human being that I had ever seen before, where I could speak to him or he to me.

And could I make that country ever seem like *home?* Some people are very much afraid all the slaves will run up North, if they are ever free. But I can assure them that they will run *back* again if they do. If I could have been assured of my freedom in Kentucky then, I would have given any thing in the world for the prospect of spending my life among my old acquaintances, and where I first saw the sky, and the sun rise and go down. It was a long time before I could make the sun work right at all. It would rise in the wrong place, and go down wrong, and finally it behaved so bad, I thought it could not be the same sun.

There was a little something added to this feeling of strangeness. I could not forget all the horrid stories slaveholders tell about Canada. They assure the slave, that when they get hold of slaves in Canada, they make various uses of them. Sometimes they *skin* the *head*, and wear the wool on their coat collars — put them into the lead mines with both eyes out — the young slaves they eat — and as for the Red Coats, they are sure death to the slave. However ridiculous to a well informed person such stories may appear, they work powerfully upon the excited imagination of an ignorant slave. With these stories all fresh in mind, when I arrived at St. Thomas, I kept a bright look out for the Red Coats. As I was turning the corner of one of the streets. sure enough, there stood before me a *Red Coat* in full uniform, with his tall bear-skin cap a foot and a half high, his gun shouldered, and he standing as erect as a guide-post. Sure enough, that is the fellow that they tell about catching the slave. I turned on my heel and sought another street. On turning another corner, the *same* soldier, as I thought, faced me with his black cap and stern look. Sure enough, my time has come now. I was as near scared to death then, as a man can be and breathe. I could not have felt any worse, if he had shot me right through the heart. I made off again as soon as I dared to move. I inquired for a tavern. When I came up to it, there was a great brazen lion sleeping over the door, and although I knew it was not alive, I had been so well frightened, that I was almost afraid to go in. Hunger drove me to it at last, and I asked for something to eat.

On my way to St. Thomas I was also badly frightened. A man asked me who I was. I was afraid to tell him, a runaway slave, lest he should have me to the mines. I was afraid to say, "I am an American," lest he should shoot me, for I knew there had been trouble between the British and Americans. I inquired at length for the place where the greatest number of colored soldiers were. I was told there were a great many at New London; so for New London I started. I got a ride with some country people to the latter place. They asked me who I was, and I told them from Kentucky; and they, in a familiar way, called me "Old Kentuck." I saw some soldiers on the way, and asked the men what they had soldiers for. They said they were kept "to get *drunk* and be *whipt;*" that was the chief use they made of them. At last I reached New London, and here I found soldiers in great numbers. I attended at their parade, and saw the guard driving the people back; but it required no guard to keep me off. I thought, if you will let me alone, I will not trouble you. I was as much afraid of a red coat, as I would have been of a bear. Here I asked again for the colored soldiers. The answer was, "Out at Chatham, about seventy miles distant." I started for Chatham. The first night I stopped at a place called the Indian Settlement. The door was barred at the house where I was, which I did not like so well, as I was yet somewhat afraid of their Canadian tricks. Just before I got to Chatham, I met two colored soldiers, with a white man bound, and driving him along before them. This was something quite new. I thought then, sure enough this is the land for me. I had seen a great many colored people bound, and in the hands of the whites, but this was changing things right about. This removed all my suspicions, and ever after I felt quite easy in Canada. I made diligent inquiry for several slaves that I had known in Kentucky, and at length found one named Henry. He told me of several others with whom I had been acquainted, and from him also I received the first correct information about brother Milton. I knew that he had left Kentucky about a year before I did, and I supposed, until now, that he was in Canada. Henry told me he was at Oberlin, Ohio.

At Chatham I hired myself for a while to recruit my purse a little, as it had become pretty well drained by this

4 *

time. I had only about sixty-four dollars when I left
Kentucky, and I had been living upon it now for about
six weeks. Mr. Everett, with whom I worked, treated me
kindly, and urged me to stay in Canada, offering me business on his farm. He declared "there was no 'free state'
in America, all were *slave* states — bound to slavery, and
the slave could have no asylum in any of them." There
is certainly a great deal of truth in this remark. I have
felt, wherever I may be in the United States, the kidnappers may be upon me at any moment. If I should creep
up to the top of the monument on Bunker's Hill, beneath
which my father fought, I should not be safe even there.
The slave-mongers have a right, by the laws of the United
States, to seek me even upon the top of the monument,
whose base rests upon the bones of those who fought for
freedom.

I soon after made my way to Sandwich, and crossed
over to Detroit, on my way to Ohio, to see Milton. While
in Canada I swapped away my pistol. as I thought I
should not need it, for an old watch. When I arrived at
Detroit, I found my watch was gone. I put my baggage,
with nearly every cent of money I had. on board the boat
for Cleveland, and went back to Sandwich to search for
the old watch. The ferry here was about three-fourths of
a mile, and in my zeal for the old watch, I wandered so
far that I did not get back in season for the boat, and had
the satisfaction of hearing her *last* bell just as I was about
to leave the Canada shore. When I got back to Detroit
I was in a fine fix; my money and my clothes gone, and
I left to wander about in the streets of Detroit. A man
may be a man for all clothes or money, but he don't feel
quite so well, any how. What to do now I could hardly

tell. It was about the first of November. I wandered about and picked up something very cheap for supper, and paid ninepence for lodging. All the next day no boat for Cleveland. Long days and nights to me. At length another boat was up for Cleveland. I went to the captain to tell him my story; he was very cross and savage — said a man no business from home without money — that so many told stories about losing money that he did not know what to believe. He finally asked me how much money I had. I told him sixty-two and a half cents. Well, he said, give me that, and pay the balance when you get there. I gave him every cent I had. We were a day and a night on the passage, and I had nothing to eat except some cold potatoes, which I picked from a barrel of fragments, and cold victuals. I went to the steward, or cook, and asked for something to eat, but he told me his orders were strict to give away nothing, and if he should do it, he would lose his place at once.

When the boat came to Cleveland it was in the night, and I thought I would spend the balance of the night in the boat. The steward soon came along, and asked if I did not know that the boat had landed, and the passengers had gone ashore. I told him I knew it, but I had paid the captain all the money I had, and could get no shelter for the night unless I remained in the boat. He was very harsh and unfeeling, and drove me ashore, although it was very cold, and snow on the ground. I walked around awhile, till I saw a light in a small house of entertainment. I called for lodging. In the morning, the Frenchman, who kept it, wanted to know if I would have breakfast. I told him no. He said then I might pay for my lodging. I told him I would do so before I left, and that my outside coat might hang there till I paid him.

I was obliged at once to start on an expedition for raising *some cash*. My resources were not very numerous. I took a *hair* brush that I had paid three York shillings for, a short time before, and sallied out to make a sale. But the wants of every person I met seemed to be in the same direction with my own; they wanted *money* more than hair brushes. At last I found a customer who paid me ninepence *cash*, and a small balance in the shape of something to eat for breakfast. I was started square for that day, and delivered out of my present distress. But hunger will return, and all the quicker when a man don't know how to satisfy it when it does come. I went to a plain boarding house, and told the man just my situation, that I was waiting for the boat to return from Buffalo, hoping to get my baggage and money. He said he would board me two or three days and risk it. I tried to get work, but no one seemed inclined to employ me. At last I gave up in despair, about my luggage, and concluded to start as soon as possible for Oberlin. I sold my great coat for two dollars, paid one for my board, and with the other I was going to pay my fare to Oberlin. That night, after I had made all my arrangements to leave in the morning, the boat came. On hearing the bell of a steam boat, in the night, I jumped up and went to the wharf, and found my baggage; paid a quarter of a dollar for the long journey it had been carried, and glad enough to get it again at that.

The next morning I took the stage for Oberlin; found several abolitionists from that place in the coach. They mentioned a slave named Milton Clarke, who was living there, that he had a brother in Canada, and that he expected him there soon. They spoke in a very friendly manner of Milton, and of the slaves; so after we had had a long conversation, and I perceived they were all friendly, I made myself known to them. To be thus surrounded at once with friends, in a land of strangers, was something quite new to me. The impression made by the kindness of these strangers upon my heart, will never be effaced. I thought there must be some new principle at work here, such as I had not seen much of in Kentucky. That evening I arrived at Oberlin, and found Milton boarding at a Mrs. Cole's. Finding here so many friends, my first impression was that all the abolitionists in the country must live right there together. When Milton spoke of going to Massachusetts, "No" said I, "we better stay here where the *abolitionists* live." And when they assured me that the friends of the slave were more numerous in Massachusetts than in Ohio, I was greatly surprised.

Milton and I had not seen each other for a year; during that time we had passed through the greatest change in outward condition, that can befal a man in this world. How glad we were to greet each other in what we then *thought* a *free* State, may be easily imagined. We little dreamed of the dangers sleeping around us. Brother Milton had not encountered so much danger in getting away as I had. But his time for suffering was soon to come. For several years before his escape, Milton had hired his time of his master, and had been employed as a steward in different steam boats upon the river. He had paid as high as two hundred dollars a year for his time. From his master he had a written pass, permitting him to go up and down the Mississippi and Ohio rivers when he pleased. He found it easy therefore to land on the north side of the Ohio river, and concluded to take his own time for returning. He had caused a letter to be written to Mr. L., his pretended owner, telling him to give himself no anxiety on his account ; that he had found by experience he had wit enough to take care of himself, and he thought the care of his master was not worth the two hundred dollars a year which he had been paying for it for four years ; that on the whole, if his master would be quiet and contented, he thought he should do very well.   This letter, the escape of two persons belonging to the same family, and from the same region, in one year, waked up the fears and the *spite* of the slave holders.   However, they let us have a little respite, and through the following winter and spring, we were employed in various kinds of work at Oberlin and in the neighborhood.

All this time I was deliberating upon a plan by which to go down and rescue Cyrus, our youngest brother, from bondage.   In July 1842, I gathered what little money I had saved, which was not a large sum, and started for Kentucky again.   As near as I remember I had about twenty dollars.   I did not tell my plan to but one or two at Oberlin, because there were many slaves there, and I did not know but that it might get to Kentucky in some way through them sooner than I should.   On my way down through Ohio, I advised with several well known friends of the slave.   Most of them pointed out the dangers I should encounter, and urged me not to go.   One young man told me to go, and the God of heaven would prosper me.   I knew it was dangerous, but I did not then dream of all that I must suffer in body and mind before I was through with it.   It is not a very comfortable feeling to be creeping round day and night for nearly two weeks together in a den of lions, where if one of them happens to put his paw on you, it is certain death. or something much worse.

At Ripley, I met a man who had lived in Kentucky; he encouraged me to go forward, and directed me about the roads. He told me to keep on a back route not much travelled, and I should not be likely to be molested. I crossed the river at Ripley, and when I reached the other side, and was again upon the soil on which I had suffered so much, I *trembled, shuddered,* at the thoughts of what might happen to me. My fears, my feelings overcame for the moment all my resolution, and I was for a time completely overcome with emotion. Tears flowed like a brook of water. I had just left kind friends; I was now where every man I met would be my enemy. It was a long time before I could summon courage sufficient to proceed. I had with me a rude map made by the Kentuckian whom I saw at Ripley. After examining this as well as I could, I proceeded. In the afternoon of the first day, as I was sitting in a stream to bathe and cool my feet, a man rode up on horseback, and entered into a long conversation with me. He asked me some questions about my travelling, but none but what I could easily answer. He pointed out to me a house where a white woman lived, who he said had recently suffered terribly from a fright. Eight slaves, that were running away, called for something to eat, and the poor woman was sorely scared by them. For his part, the man said, he hoped they never would find the slaves again. Slavery was the curse of Kentucky. He had been brought up to work and he liked to work, but slavery made it it disgraceful for any white man to work. From this conversation I was almost a good mind to trust this man, and tell him my story, but on second thought, I concluded it might be just as *safe* not to do it. A hundred or two dollars for returning a slave, for a poor man, is a heavy temptation. At night

I stopped at the house of a widow woman,—not a tavern exactly, but they often entertained people there. The next day when I got as far as Cynthiana, within about twenty miles of Lexington, I was sore all over and lame from having walked so far. I tried to hire a horse and carriage to help me a few miles. At last I agreed with a man to send me forward to a certain place, which he said was twelve miles, and for which I paid him, in advance, three dollars. It proved to be only seven miles. This was now Sabbath day, as I had selected that as the most suitable day for making my entrance into Lexington. There is much more passing in and out on that day, and I thought I should be much less observed than on any other day.

When I approached the city and met troops of idlers on foot and on horseback, sauntering out of the city, I was very careful to keep my umbrella before my face, as people passed, and kept my eyes right before me. There were many persons in the place, who had known me, and I did not care to be recognized by any of them. Just before entering the city, I turned off to the field, and laid down under a tree and waited for night. When its curtains were fairly over me, I started up, took two pocket handkerchiefs, tied one over my forehead, the other under my chin, and marched forward for the city. It was not then so dark as I wished it was. I met a young slave driving cows. He was quite disposed to condole with me, and said, in a very sympathetic manner, " Massa sick." " Yes, boy," I said, " Massa sick, — drive along your cows." The next colored man I met, I knew him in a moment, but he did not recognize me. I made for the wash-house of the man with whom Cyrus lived. I reached it without attracting any notice, and found there an old slave as true as steel. I inquired for Cyrus, he said he was at home. He very soon recollected me ; and while the boy was gone to call Cyrus, he uttered a great many exclamations of wonder to think I should return.

"Good heaven, boy! what you back here for? What on arth you here for, my son? O! I scared for you! They kill you, just as sure as I alive, if they catch you! Why, in name of Liberty, didn't you stay away, when you gone so slick! Sartin, I never did 'spect to see you again!" I said, Don't be scared. But he kept repeating, "I scared for you! I scared for you!" When I told him my errand, his wonder was somewhat abated, but still his exclamations were repeated all the evening. "What brought you back here?" In a few minutes Cyrus made his appearance, filled with little less of wonder than the old man had manifested. I had intended, when I left him about a year before, that I would return for him, if I was successful in my effort for freedom. He was very glad to see me, and entered with great animation upon the plan for his own escape. He had a wife, who was a free woman, and consequently he had a home. He soon went out, and left me in the wash-room with the old man. He went home to apprize his wife, and to prepare a room for my concealment. His wife is a very active, industrious woman, and they were enabled to rent a very comfortable house, and at this time had a spare room in the attic, where I could be thoroughly concealed.

He soon returned, and said every thing was ready. I went home with him, and before ten o'clock at night I was stowed away in a little room that was to be my prison-house for about a week. It was a comfortable room ; still the confinement was close, and I was unable to take exercise, lest the people in the other part of the house should hear. I got out and walked around a little in the evening, but suffered a good deal for want of more room to live and move in. During the day Cyrus was busy making arrangements for his departure. He had several little sums of money in the hands of the foreman of the tanyard, and in other hands. Now it would not do to go right boldly up and demand his pay of every one that owed him; this would lead to suspicion at once. So he contrived various ways to get in his little debts. He had seen the foreman one day counting out some singular coin of some foreign nation; he pretended to take a great liking to that foreign money, and told the man, if he would pay him what was due him in *that* money, he would give him two or three dollars. From another person he took an order on a store, and so, in various ways, he got in his little debts as well as he could. At night we contrived to plan the ways and means of escaping. Cyrus had never been much accustomed to walking, and he dreaded very much to undertake such a journey. He proposed to take a couple of horses, as he thought he had richly earned them, over and above all he had received. I objected to this, because, if we were caught, either in Kentucky or out of it, they would bring against us the charge of stealing, and this would be far worse than the charge of running away.

To all these propositions I firmly replied, " We must go on foot." In the course of a week, Cyrus had gathered something like twenty dollars, and we were ready for our journey. A family lived in the same house with Cyrus, in a room below. How to get out in the early part of the evening, and not be discovered, was not an easy question. Finally, we agreed that Cyrus should go down and get into conversation with them, while I slipped out with his bundle of clothes, and repaired to a certain street, where he was to meet me.

As I passed silently out at the door, Cyrus was cracking his best jokes, and raising a general laugh, which completely covered my retreat. Cyrus soon took quiet and unexpected leave of his friends in that family, and leave also of his wife above — for a short time only. At a little past eight of the clock, we were beyond the bounds of the city. His wife did all she could to assist him in his effort to gain his inalienable rights. She did not dare, however, to let the slaveholders know that she knew any thing of his attempt to run away. He had told the slaves that he was going to see his sister, about twelve miles off. It was Saturday night when we left Lexington. On entering the town, when I went in, I was so intent upon covering up my face, that I took but little notice of the roads. We were very soon exceedingly perplexed to know what road to take. The moon favored us, for it was a clear, beautiful night. On we came, but at the cross of the roads what to do we did not know. At length I climbed one of the guide posts, and *spelled* out the names as well as I could. We were on the road to freedom's boundary, and with a strong step we measured off the path ; but again the cross roads perplexed us. This time we took hold of the sign post and lifted it out of the ground, and turned it upon one of its horns, and spelled out the way again. As we started from this goal, I told Cyrus we had not put up the sign post. He pulled forward, and said he guessed we would do that when we came back. Whether the sign board is up or down, we have never been there to see.

Soon after leaving the city, we met a great many of the patrols, but they did not arrest us, and we had no disposition to trouble them.

While we were pressing on by moon light, and sometimes in great doubt about the road, Cyrus was a good deal discouraged. He thought if we got upon the wrong road, it would be almost certain death for us, or something worse. In the morning we found that, on account of our embarrassment in regard to the roads, we had only made a progress of some twenty or twenty-five miles. But we were greatly cheered to find they were so many miles in the right direction. Then we put the best foot forward, and urged our way as fast as possible. In the afternoon it rained very hard, the roads were muddy and slippery. We had slept none the night before, and had been of course very much excited. In this state of mind and of body, just before dark we stopped in a little patch of bushes, to discuss the expediency of going to a house, which we saw at a distance, to spend the night.

As we sat there, Cyrus became very much excited, and pointing across the road, exclaimed, "Don't you see that animal there." I looked, but saw nothing; still he affirmed that he saw a dreadful-looking animal looking at us, and ready to make a spring. He began to feel for his pistols, but I told him not to fire there; but he persisted in pointing to the animal, although I am persuaded he saw nothing, only by the force of his imagination. I had some doubts about telling this story, lest people would not believe me; but a friend has suggested to me that such things are not uncommon, when the imagination is strongly excited. The reader may see confirmation of this fact, by turning to a note at the end of this pamphlet.

In travelling through the rain and mud this afternoon, we suffered beyond all power of description. Sometimes we found ourselves just ready to stand fast asleep in the middle of the road. Our feet were blistered all over. When Cyrus would get almost discouraged, I urged him on, saying we were walking for *freedom now*. Yes, he would say, "Freedom is good, Lewis, but this is a *hard*, *h-a-r-d* way to get it." This he would say half asleep. We were so weak before night, that we several times fell upon our knees in the road. We had crackers with us, but we had no appetite to eat — *fears* were behind us, *hope* before—and we were driven and drawn as hard as ever men were. Our limbs and joints were so stiff, that if we took a step to the right hand or left, it seemed as though it would shake us to pieces. It was a dark, weary day to us both.

At length I succeeded in getting the consent of Cyrus to go to a house for the night. We found a plain farmer's family. The good man was all taken up in talking about the camp-meeting held that day about three miles from his house. He only asked us where we were from, and we told him our home was in Ohio. He said the young men had behaved unaccountably bad at the camp-meeting, and they had but little comfort of it. They mocked the preachers, and disturbed the meeting badly.

We escaped suspicion more readily, as I have no doubt, from the supposition, on the part of many, that we were going to the camp-meeting. Next morning we called at the meeting, as it was on our way, bought up a little extra gingerbread against the time of need, and marched forward for the Ohio. When any one inquired why we left the meeting so soon, we had an answer ready : the young men behave so bad, we can get no good of the meeting.

5*

By this time we limped badly, and we were sore all over. A young lady whom we met, noticing that we walked lame, cried out, mocking us, "O my feet, my feet, how sore." At about eleven o'clock we reached the river, two miles below Ripley. The boatman was on the other side. We called for him. He asked us a few questions. This was a last point with us. We tried our best to appear unconcerned. I asked questions about the boats, as though I had been there before; went to Cyrus and said, Sir, I have no change, will you lend me enough to pay my toll? I will pay you before we part. When we were fairly landed upon the northern bank, and had gone a few steps, Cyrus stopped suddenly on seeing the water gush out at the side of the hill. Said he, "Lewis, give me that tin cup." What in the world do you want of a tin cup now? we have not time to stop. The cup he would have. Then he went up to the spring, dipped and drank, and dipped and drank; then he would look round and drink again. "What in the world," said I, "are you fooling there for?" "O," said he, "this is the first time I ever had a chance to drink water that ran out of the *free* dirt." Then we went a little further, and he sat down on a log. I urged him forward. "O," said he, "I must sit on this free timber a little while."

A short distance further on, we saw a man who seemed to watch us very closely. I asked him which was the best way to go, *over* the hill before us or *around* it. I did this to appear to know something about the location. He went off without offering any obstacles to our journey. In going up the hill, Cyrus would stop and lay down and roll over. "What in the world are you about, Cyrus; don't you see Kentucky is over there?" He still continued to roll and kiss the ground; said it was a game horse that could roll clear over; — then he would put face to the ground, and roll over and over. "First time," he said, "he ever rolled on *free* grass."

After he recovered a little from his sportive mood, we went up to the house of a good friend of the slave at Ripley. We were weary and worn enough; though ever since we left the River, it seemed as though Cyrus was young and spry as a colt; but when we got where we could *rest*, we found ourselves *tired*. The good lady showed us into a good bed-room. Cyrus was skittish. He would not go in and lay down. "I am afraid," said he, "of old mistress. She is too good — too good — can't be so — they want to catch us both." So to pacify him, I had to go out into the orchard and rest there. When the young men came home, he soon got acquainted, and felt sure they were his friends. From this place we were sent on by the friends, from place to place, till we reached Oberlin, Ohio, — in about five weeks after I left there to go for Cyrus. I had encountered a good deal of peril; had suffered much from anxiety of feeling; but felt richly repaid in seeing another brother free.

We stopped at Oberlin a few days, and then Cyrus started for Canada. He did not feel exactly safe. When he reached the Lake, he met a man from Lexington who knew him perfectly; indeed, the very man of whom his wife hired her house. This man asked him if he was free. He told him yes, he was free, and he was hunting for brother Milton, to get him to go back and settle with the old man for his freedom. Putnam told him that was all right. He asked Cyrus if he should still want that house his wife lived in? "O yes," said Cyrus, "we will notify

you when we don't want it any more. You tell them I
shall be down there in a few days. I have heard of Milton, and expect to have him soon to carry back with me."
Putnam went home, and when he found what a fool Cyrus
had made of him, he was vexed enough. "A rascal,"
he said, "I could have caught him as well as not."

Cyrus hastened over to Canada. He did not like that
country so well as the States, and in a few weeks returned. He had already sent a letter to his wife, giving her an
account of his successful escape, and urging her to join
him as soon as possible. He had the pleasure of meeting
his wife and her three children by a former husband, and
they have found a quiet resting place, where, if the rumor
of oppression reaches them, they do not feel its scourge,
nor its chains. And there is no doubt entertained by any
of his friends but he can take care of himself.

He begins already to appreciate his rights, and to main-
tain them as a freeman. The following paragraph concerning him was published in the Liberty Press about one
year since.

PROGRESS OF FREEDOM.

SCENE AT HAMILTON VILLAGE, N. Y.

Mr. Cyrus Clarke, a brother of the well known Milton and
Lewis Clarke, (all of whom, till within a short time since, for
some twenty-five years were slaves in Kentucky,) mildly, but
firmly presented his ballot at the town meeting board. Be it
known that said Cyrus, as well as his brothers, are *white*, with
only a sprinkling of the African—just enough to make them
bright, quick, and intelligent, and scarcely observable in the
color except by the keen and scenting slaveholder. Mr. Clarke
had all the necessary qualifications of white men to vote.

Slave.—Gentlemen, here is my ballot, I wish to vote. (Board and bystanders, well knowing him, all were aghast — the waters were troubled — the slave legions were " up in their might.")

Judge E.—You can't vote ! Are you not, and have you not been a slave ?

Slave.—I shall not *lie* to vote. I am and have been a slave, so called ; but I wish to vote, and I believe it my right and duty.

Judge E.—Slaves can't vote.

Slave.—Will you just show me in your books, constitution, or whatever you call them, where it says a slave can't vote ?

Judge E.—(Pretending to look over the law, &c., well knowing he was " used up.") Well, well, you are a colored man. and can't vote without you are worth $250.

Slave.— I am as white as *you ;* and don't *you vote !*

(Mr. E. is well known to be very dark ; indeed, as dark or darker than Clarke. The current began to set against Mr. E. by murmurs, sneers, laughs, and many other demonstrations of dislike.)

Judge E. — Are you not a *colored man ?* and is not your hair curly ?

Slave. — We are both colored men ; and all we differ is, that you have not the handsome wavy curl ; you raise *Goat's wool,* and I come, as you see, a little nearer *Saxony.*

At this time the fire and fun was at its height, and was fast consuming the judge with public opprobrium.

Judge E. — I challenge this man's vote, he being a colored man, and not worth $250.

Friends and foes warmly contested what constituted a colored man by the New York statute. The board finally came to the honorable conclusion that, to be a *colored* man, he must be at least one half blood African. Mr. Clarke, the SLAVE, then voted, he being nearly full white. I have the history of this transaction from Mr. Clarke, in person. In substance it is as told me, but varying more or less from his language used.

Paris, March 12, 1841. J. THOMPSON.

Martha, the wife of Cyrus, had a long story of the wrath of the slaveholders, because he ran away. Monday morning she went down in great distress to the overseer to inquire for her husband. She, of course, was in great anxiety about him, Mr. Logan threatened her severely, but she, having a little mixture of the Indian, Saxon and African blood, was quite too keen for them. She succeeded in so far lulling their suspicions as to make her escape, and was very fortunate in her journey to her husband.

Soon after the escape of Cyrus, the Goths and Vandals of Kentucky made an irruption into Ohio, going about like Satan, seeking whom they might devour. Their special object of attack, however, was brother Milton. In August 1842, Milton and myself went up to Madison, Lake county, Ohio, to spend a few days. Milton went in a private conveyance with a widow lady named Cole, and her daughter. I went in the stage. Mrs. Cole and daughter spent their time at Dr. Merriam's. Milton and myself were the guests of a Mr. Winchester. We went to meeting with the family on the Sabbath, and in the evening gave some account of our sufferings while in bondage. *Postlewaite* and McGowan, two pirates from Kentucky, were in the neighborhood at this time, waiting like beasts of prey to leap upon their victim.

Monday morning, my brother and myself, with two or three of Mr. Winchester's family, rode up to Dr. Merriam's to see the sick daughter of Mrs. Cole. Milton sat a few moments in the carriage, and the sick daughter of Mrs. Cole and a child of Dr. Merriam came out and wanted a ride. He had driven only a mile or two, when a close carriage met him, and turning directly across the road, several persons leaped out and stopped his horse. He had no suspicion who they were, and asked what they wanted. If they wanted money, he had but half a dollar, he told them, and they were welcome to that. They replied, " We do not want your money, but you." Four men were now around him, and one of them ordered him to get out of the buggy — "Have you we will, dead or alive."

As he jumped from the carriage, and struck the ground, they all leaped upon him, bent his head down to the ground, and bound him with a rope. The horse, which he left turned out of the road, upset the carriage, and tipped out the little girls; the sick one never recovered from the shock she received. Milton appealed to them to take care of the children, who were screaming in a frightful manner. The only reply was, that if they did not hold their tongues, they would cut their d———d throats.

After Milton was bound, he was carried to Centreville, before a magistrate called Page. The agents of Mr. Logan of Kentucky, had power of attorney to seize and bring home, wherever found, one Milton Clarke, the property of the said Logan. These man-hunters were provided with papers, by which they could identify him, and had also recommendations from some of the leading men in Kentucky. They employed a miserable toad-eater of a lawyer, who calls himself Robert Harper. This less than man was ready to betray innocent blood for less than thirty pieces of silver. The examination was continued before the magistrate for several hours. The result was, that Milton was delivered over to those whose tender mercies are cruel. Meanwhile, the friends of the slave had not been idle. They had procured two writs, one from Lake county, to arrest Postlewaite & Co. as kidnappers, another from Ashtabula county, to take the body of Milton Clarke.

The road that lead from the place of trial was between the two counties. Great numbers were by this time gathered together. They so managed to throw obstructions in the way of the carriage, that it could make only a zigzag course until both writs were served, Milton was released and taken into Ashtabula county and permitted to go free, the kidnappers in great wrath were taken in an opposite direction, and after a while they were permitted to return empty handed to Kentucky.

We remained but a short time after this in Ohio. I spent a few days in New York; found there a great many warm friends, and in the autumn of 1843 I came to old Massachusetts. Since that time I have been engaged a large part of the time in telling the story of what I have felt and seen of slavery.

I have generally found large audiences, and a great desire to hear about slavery. I have been in all the New-England States except Connecticut. Have held, I suppose, more than five hundred meetings in different places, sometimes two or three in a place. These meetings have been kindly noticed by many of the papers of all parties and sects. Others have been very bitter and unjust in their remarks, and tried to throw every possible obstacle in my way. A large majority of ministers have been willing to give notice of my meetings, and many of them have attended them. I find that most ministers say they are abolitionists, but truth compels me to add, that in talking with them, I find many are more zealous to apologize for the slave-holders, than they are to take any active measures to do away slavery.

Since coming to the free States, I have been struck with great surprise at the quiet and peaceable manner in which

families live. I had no conception that *women* could live
without quarreling, till I came into the free States.

After I had been in Ohio a short time, and had not seen
nor heard any scolding or quarreling in the families where
I was, I did not know how to account for it. I told Milton, one day, what a faculty these women have of keeping
all their bad feelings to themselves. I have not seen them
quarrel with their husbands, nor with the girls, or children,
since I have been here. " O," said Milton, " these women
are not like our women in Kentucky ; they don't fight at
all." I told him I doubted that ; I guess they do it somewhere — in the kitchen, or down cellar. " It can't be,"
said I, " that a woman can live, and not scold or quarrel."
Milton laughed, and told me to watch them, and see if I
could catch them at it. I have kept my eyes and ears
open from that day to this, and I have not found the place
where the women get mad and rave like they do in Kentucky yet. If they do it here, they are uncommon sly ;
but I have about concluded that they are altogether different here from what they are in the slave States. I reckon
slavery must work upon their minds and dispositions, and
make them ugly.

It has been a matter of great wonder to me also, to see
all the children, rich and poor, going to school. Every
few miles I see a school-house here ; I did not know what
it meant when I saw these houses, when I first came to
Ohio. In Kentucky, if you should feed your horse only
when you come to a school-house, he would starve to death.

I never had heard a church bell only at Lexington, in
my life. When I saw steeples and meeting houses so
thick, it seemed like I had got into another world. Nothing seems more wonderful to me now, than the different

6

way they keep the Sabbath there, and here.   In the
country, in summer, there the people gather in groups
around the meeting house, *built of logs,* or around in the
groves where they often meet ; one company, and perhaps
the minister with them, are talking about the price of
niggers, pork, and corn ; another group are playing cards ;
others are swapping horses, or horse-racing ; all in sight of
the meeting-house or place of worship.   After a while the
minister tells them it is time to begin.   They stop playing
and talking for awhile.   If they call him right smart, they
hear him out ; if he is "no account," they turn to their
cards and horses, and finish their devotion in this manner.

The slaveholders are continually telling how poor the
white people are in the free States, and how much they
suffer from poverty — no masters to look out for them.
When, therefore, I came into Ohio, and found nearly
every family living in more real comfort than almost any
slaveholder, you may easily see I did not know what to
make of it.   I see how it is now — every man in the free
States *works ;* and as they work for themselves, they do
twice as much as they would do for another.

In fact, my wonder at the contrast between the slave
and the free States has not ceased yet.   The more I see
here, the more I *know* slavery curses the masters as well
as the slave.   It curses the soil, the houses, the churches,
the schools, the burying-grounds, the flocks and the herds ;
it curses man and beast, male and female, old and young.
It curses the child in the cradle, and heaps curses upon
upon the old man as he lies in his grave.   Let all the
people, then, of the civilized world get up upon Mount
Ebal, and curse it with a long and bitter curse, and with a
loud voice, till it withers and dies ; till the year of Jubilee

dawns upon the South, till the sun of a FREE DAY sends a beam of light and joy into every cabin.

I wish here sincerely to recognize the hand of a kind Providence in leading me from that terrible house of bondage, for raising me up friends in a land of strangers, and for leading me, as I hope, to a saving knowledge of the truth as it is in Christ. A slave cannot be sure that he will always enjoy his religion in peace. Some of them are beaten for acts of devotion. I can never express to God all the gratitude which I owe him for the many favors I now enjoy. I try to live in love with all men. Nothing would delight me more, than to take the worst slaveholder by the hand, even Mrs. Banton, and freely forgive her, if I thought she had repented of her sins. While she, or any other man or woman is trampling down the image of God, and *abusing* the life out of the poor slave, I cannot believe they are Christians, or that they ought to be allowed the Christian name for one moment. I testify against them now, as having none of the spirit of Christ. There will be a cloud of swift witnesses against them at the day of judgment. The testimony of the slave will be heard then. He has no voice at the tribunals of earthly justice, but he will one day be heard ; and then such revelations will be made, as will fully justify the opinion which I have been compelled to form of slaveholders. They are a SEED of *evil-doers*, — *corrupt* are they — they have done abominable works.

APPENDIX.

A SKETCH OF THE CLARKE FAMILY.

My mother was called a very handsome woman. She was very much esteemed by all who knew her ; — the slaves looked up to her for advice. She died, much lamented, of the cholera, in the year 1833. I was not at home, and had not even the melancholy pleasure of following her to her grave.

1. The name of the oldest member of the family was Archy. He never enjoyed very good health, but was a man of great ingenuity, and very much beloved by all his associates, colored and white. Through his own exertions, and the kindness of C. M. Clay and one or two other friends, he procured his freedom. He lived to repay Mr. Clay and others the money advanced for him, but not long enough to enjoy for many years the freedom for which he had struggled so hard. He paid six hundred dollars for himself. He died about seven years since, leaving a wife and four or five children in bondage — the inheritance of the widow and poor orphans is, LABOR WITHOUT WAGES — WRONGS WITH NO REDRESS — SEPARATION FROM EACH OTHER FOR LIFE, and no being to hear their com-

6*

plaint, but that God who is the *widow's God and Judge.*
"Shall I not be avenged on such a nation as this?"

2. Sister Christiana was next to Archy in age. She
was first married to a free colored man. By him she had
several children. Her master did not like this connection,
and her husband was driven away, and told never to be
seen there again. The name of her master is Oliver Anderson — he is a leading man in the Presbyterian Church,
and is considered one of the best among slaveholders.
Mr. Anderson married Polly Campbell, at the time I was
given to Mrs. Betsy Banton. I believe she and Mrs. Banton have not spoken together since they divided the slaves
at the death of their father. They are the only two sisters now living of the Campbell family.

3. Dennis is the third member of our family. He is a
free man in Kentucky, and is doing a very good business
there. He was assisted by a Mr. Wm. L. Stevenson, and
also by his sister, in getting his freedom. He never had
any knowledge of our intention of running away, nor did
he assist us in any manner whatever.

4. Alexander is the fourth child of my mother. He is
the slave of a Dr. Richardson; has with him a very easy
time; lives as well as a man can and be a slave; has no
intention of running away. He lives very much like a
second-hand gentleman, and I do not know as he would
leave Kentucky on any condition.

5. My mother lost her fifth child soon after it was
born.

6. Delia came next. Hers was a most bitter and tragi-
cal history. She was so unfortunate as to be uncommonly
handsome, and when arrived at woman's estate, was considered a great prize for the guilty passions of the slave-

holders. She was at this time the property of Joseph Logan, who had married one of the daughters of Mr. Campbell. On the death of his wife, he proposed to make a mistress of poor Delia. By the advice of her mother, she rejected every such proposal. Her mother urged her to die, rather than give herself up to him.

For her refusal, she was repeatedly and most cruelly whipped. One day, while beating her in a most terrible manner, my mother went out, (she was at this time the property of this same Logan,) and entreated him not to kill her child. The brute turned round and knocked her down, and beat out several of her teeth. Milton was standing by, and when he saw this, he ran to the wood-house and got an axe, and was coming to cut this monster down. Mother was up, and met him just in time to keep him back; if he had attempted it, of course Logan would have killed him in a moment.

Logan never succeeded in his infernal purposes. Vexed and disappointed, he determined on revenge. Sister was sold to Warren Orford, a slave-dealer, carried down to New Orleans, and put upon the auction block. The bidding went on rapidly, till it was up to a thousand dollars; there seemed to be some hesitation then. She had been decked out in rich clothing, like a victim for the sacrifice. The auctioneer at this point took out his recommendations — "She is a member of the Baptist Church, in good standing, pious and exemplary, and *warranted* never to have had connection with any man."

The bidding was suddenly brisk, and she was knocked off at *sixteen* hundred dollars. Fortunately, God had provided for her a humane master. She went immediately into the hands of a kind-hearted Frenchman, who emancipated her, and made her his lawful wife.

In a few years her husband died, and left her a handsome property. She only visited Kentucky once after this, when she assisted Dennis in getting his freedom. She intended to go on, and, if possible, get the whole family free, as fast as she could. But death cut short all her purposes of kindness and sisterly affection. She is remembered by the whole family with a most melancholy and tender interest. She left no children, and the estate came properly to the brother who is free in Kentucky. But he has made very little exertion to get it, and probably would not be successful if he should.*

7. To No. 7, I, Lewis Clarke, respond, and of me you have heard enough already.

8. Milton comes next, and he is speaking for himself. He is almost constantly engaged in giving lectures upon the subject of slavery; has more calls usually than he can attend to.

9. Manda, the ninth child, died when she was about fifteen or sixteen years of age. She suffered a good deal from Joseph Logan's second wife.

10. Cyrus is the youngest of the family, and lives at Hamilton, New York.

---

* She left a writing saying she wished Milton to take her property, and use it for the family. He went down to New Orleans to get it, but being a *slave*, he was told there he could not get the property.

QUESTIONS AND ANSWERS.

The following questions are often asked me, when I meet the people in public, and I have thought it would be well to put down the answers here.

How many holidays in a year do the slaves in Kentucky have? They usually have six days at Christmas, and two or three others in the course of the year. Public opinion generally seems to require this much of slaveholders; a few give more, some less, some *none*, not a day nor an hour.

How do slaves spend the Sabbath? Every way the master pleases. There are certain kinds of work which are respectable for Sabbath-day. Slaves are often sent out to salt the cattle, collect and count the pigs and sheep, mend fences, drive the stock from one pasture to another. Breaking young horses and mules to send them to market, yoking young oxen and training them, is proper Sabbath work. Piling and burning brush on the back part of the lot, grubbing brier patches that are out of the way, and where they will not be seen. Sometimes corn must be shelled in the corn-crib; hemp is baled in the hemp-house. The still-house must be attended on the Sabbath. In these and various other such like employments, the more avaricious slaveholders keep their slaves busy a good part of every Sabbath. It is a great day for visiting and eating, and the house servants often have more to do on that than on any other day.

What if strangers come along and see you at work?

We must quit shelling corn, and go to play with the cobs, or else we must be clearing land on our own account. We must cover up master's sins as much as possible, and take it all to ourselves. It is hardly fair; for he ought rather to account for our sins, than we for his.

Why did you not learn to read? I did not *dare* to learn. I attempted to spell some words when a child. One of the children of Mrs. Banton went in and told her that she heard Lewis spelling. Mrs. B. jumped up as though she had been shot. "Let me ever know you to spell another word, I'll take your *heart* right out of you." I had a strong desire to learn. But it would not do to have slaves learn to read and write. They could read the guide-boards. They could write passes for each other. They cannot leave the plantation on the Sabbath without a written pass.

What proportion of slaves attend church on the Sabbath? In the country not *more* than *one in ten on an average.*

How many slaves have you ever known that could read? I never saw more than three or four that could properly read at all. I never saw but one that could write.

What do slaves know about the Bible? They generally believe there is somewhere a real Bible, that came from God; but they frequently say the Bible now used is master's Bible, most that they hear from it being, "Servants, obey your masters."

Are families often separated? How many such cases have you personally known? *I never knew a whole family to live together, till all were grown up, in my life.* There is almost always, in every family, some one or more keen and bright, or else sullen and stubborn slave, whose influence they are afraid of on the rest of the family, and such an one must take a walking ticket to the South.

There are other causes of separation. The death of a large owner is the occasion usually of many families being broken up. Bankruptcy is another cause of separation, and the hard-heartedness of a majority of slaveholders another and a more fruitful cause than either or all the rest. *Generally* there is but little more scruple about separating families than there is with a man who keeps sheep in selling off the lambs in the fall. On one plantation where I lived, there was an old slave named Paris. He was from fifty to sixty years old, and a very honest and apparently a pious slave. A slave-trader came along one day, gathering hands for the South. The old master ordered the waiter or coachman to take Paris into the back room, *pluck out* all his grey hairs, rub his face with a greasy towel, and then had him brought forward and sold for a *young* man. His wife consented to go with him, upon a promise from the trader that they should be sold together, with their youngest child, which she carried in her arms. They left two behind them, who were only from four to six or eight years of age. The speculator collected his drove, started for the market, and before he left the State he *sold that infant child* to pay one of his tavern bills, and took the balance in cash. This was the news which came back to us, and was never disputed.

I saw one slave mother, named Lucy, with seven children, put up by an administrator for sale. At first the mother and three small children were put up together. The purchasers objected: one says, I want the woman and the babe, but not the other children; another says, I want

that little girl; and another, I want the boy. Well, says
the Administrator, I must let you have them to the best
advantage. So the children were taken away; the mother
and infant were first sold, then child after child — the
mother looking on in perfect agony; and as one child after
another came down from the auction block, they would
run, and cling weeping to her clothes. The poor mother
stood, till nature gave way; she fainted and fell, with her
child in her arms. The only sympathy she received from
most of the hard-hearted monsters who had riven her
heart-strings asunder was, "She is a d—d deceitful bitch;
I wish she was mine, I would teach her better than to cut
up such shines as that here." When she came to, she
moaned wofully, and prayed that she might die, to be re-
lieved from her sufferings.

I knew another slave named Nathan, who had a slave
woman for a wife. She was killed by hard usage. Nathan
then declared he would never have another slave wife.
He selected a free woman for a companion. His master
opposed it violently. But Nathan persevered in his
choice, and in consequence was sold to go down South.
He returned once to see his wife, and she soon after died
of grief and disappointment. On his return South, he
leaped from the boat, and attempted to swim ashore; his
master, on board the boat, took a gun and deliberately
shot him, and he drifted down the current of the river.

On this subject of separation of families, I must plant
one more rose in the garland that I have already tied
upon the brow of the sweet Mrs. Banton. The reader
cannot have forgotten her; and in the delectable business
of tearing families asunder she of course would have a
hand. A slave by the name of Susan was taken by Mrs.

Banton on mortgage. She had been well treated where she was brought up, had a husband, and they were very happy together. Susan mourned in bitterness over her separation, and pined away under the cruel hand of Mrs. Banton. At length she ran away, and hid herself in the neighborhood of her husband. When this came to the knowledge of Mrs. B., she charged her husband to go for "Suke," and never let her see his face unless she was with him. "No, said she, if you are offered a double price, don't you take it. I want my satisfaction out of her, and then you may sell her as soon as you please." Susan was brought back in fetters, and Mr. and Mrs. B. both took their *satisfaction;* they beat and tortured poor Susan till her premature offspring perished, and she almost sank beneath their merciless hands, and then they sold her to be carried a hundred miles farther away from her husband. Ah! slavery is like running the dissecting knife around the heart, among all the tender fibres of our being.

A man by the name of Bill Myers, in Kentucky, went to a large number of auctions, and purchased women about forty years old, with their youngest children in their arms. As they are about to cease bearing at that age, they are sold cheap. The children he took and shut up in a log pen, and set some old worn-out slave women to make broth and feed them. The mothers he gathered in a large drove, and carried them South and sold them. He was detained there for months longer than he expected, and winter coming on, and no proper provision having been made for the children, many of them perished with cold and hunger, some were frost bitten, and all were emaciated to skeletons. This was the only attempt that I ever knew, for gathering young children together, like a litter

7

of pigs, to be raised for the market.   The success was not such as to warrant a repetition on the part of Myers.

Jockey Billy Barnett had a slave-prison, where he gathered his droves of husbands, fathers and wives, separated from their friends, and he tried to keep up their spirits by employing one or two fiddlers to play for them, while they danced over and upon the torn-off fibres of their hearts. Several women were known to have died in that worse than Calcutta Black Hole of grief.   They mourned for their children, and would not be comforted because they were not.

How are the slave cabins usually built?   They are made of small logs, about from ten to twenty feet square. The roof is covered with splits, and *dirt* is thrown in to raise the bottom, and then it is beat down hard for a floor. The chimneys are made of cut sticks and clay.   In the corners, or at the sides, there are pens made, filled with straw, for sleeping.   Very commonly two or three families are huddled together in one cabin, and in cold weather they sleep together promiscuously, old and young.   Some few families are indulged in the privilege of having a few hens or ducks around them, but this is not very common.

What amount of food do slaves have in Kentucky? They are not put on allowance; they generally have enough of corn bread, and meat and soup are dealt to them occasionally.

What is the clothing of a slave for a year?   For summer he has usually a pair of tow and linen pants, and two shirts of the same material.   He has a pair of shoes, a pair of woolsey pants, and a round jacket for winter.

The account current of a slave with his master stands about thus:

ICHABOD LIVE-WITHOUT-WORK, *in account with*
                    JOHN WORK-WITHOUT-PAY, *Cr.*

To one man's work, ... $100 00

CONTRA CREDIT.

By 13 bushels of corn meal at 10 cents, . $1 30
" 100 lbs. mean bacon and pork at 1½ cents, 1 50
" Chickens, pigs, &c., taken without leave, say 1 50
" 9 yds. of tow and linen, for shirts and pants,
     at 12½, . . 1 12½
" 1 pair of shoes, ... 1 50
" Cloth for jacket and winter pants, 5½ yds. at
     2 shillings, . . 1 84
" Making clothes, . · . . . 1 00
" 1 Blanket, ... 1 00
" 2 Hats or caps, ... 75
           ——— $11 51½

            $88 48½

The account stands unbalanced thus till the great day of reckoning comes.

Now allow that one half of the slaves are capable of labor — that they can earn on an average one half the sum above named; that would give us $50 a year for 1,500,000 slaves, which would be *seventy-five millions* as *the sum robbed* from the slaves every year!! " Wo unto him that useth his neighbor's service without wages." Wo unto him that buildeth his house by iniquity, "for the stone shall cry out of the wall, and the beam out of the timber shall answer it." " Behold the hire of the laborers who have reaped down your fields, which is of you kept back by fraud, crieth; and the cries of them which have reaped are entered into the ears of the Lord of Sabaoth.

Ye have lived in pleasure on the earth and been wanton; ye have *nourished your hearts as in a day of slaughter.*"

Have you ever known a slave mother to kill her own children? There was a slave mother near where I lived, who took her child into the cellar and killed it. She did it to prevent being separated from her child. Another slave mother took her three children and threw them into a well, and then jumped in with them, and they were all drowned. Other instances I have frequently heard of. At the death of many and many a slave child I have seen the two feelings struggling in the bosom of a mother — joy that it was beyond the reach of the slave monsters, and the natural grief of a mother over her child. In the presence of the master, grief seems to predominate; when away from them, they rejoice that there is one whom the slave-driver will never torment.

How is it that masters *kill* their slaves, when they are worth so much money? They do it to gratify passion; this must be done, cost what it may. Some say a man will not kill a horse worth a hundred dollars, much less a slave worth several hundred dollars. A horse has no such *will* of his own, as the slave has — he does not provoke the man as a slave does. The master knows there is *contrivance* with the slave to outwit him — the horse has no such contrivance. This conflict of the *two* WILLS is what makes the master so much more passionate with his slave than with a horse. A slaveholder must be master on the plantation, or he knows the *example* would destroy all authority.

What do they do with old slaves who are past labor? Contrive all ways to keep them at work till the last hour of life. Make them shell corn and pack tobacco. They hunt and drive them as long as there is any life in them. Sometimes they turn them out to do the best they can, or die. One man, on moving to Missouri, sold an old slave for one dollar, to a man not worth a cent. The old slave was turned out to do the best he could; he fought with age and starvation awhile, but was soon found, one morning, *starved* to death, out of doors, and half eaten up by animals. I have known several cases where slaves were left to starve to death in old age. Generally they sell them South and let them die there; send them, I mean, before they get very old.

What makes them wash slaves in salt and water after they whip them? For two reasons; one is to make them smart, and another to prevent mortification in the lacerated flesh. I have seen men and women both washed after they had been cruelly beaten. *I have done it with my own hands.* It was the hardest work I ever did. The flesh would crawl and creep and quiver under my hands. This slave's name was Tom. He had not started his team Sunday morning early enough. The neighbors *saw* that Mr. Banton had work done on the Sabbath. Dalton, the overseer, attempted to whip him. Tom knocked him down and trod on him, and then ran away. The patrols caught him, and he was whipped *three hundred* lashes. Such a back I never saw — such work I pray that I may never do again.

Do not slaves often say that they love their masters very much? Say so? yes, certainly. And this loving master and mistress is the hardest work that slaves have to do. When any stranger is present we have to love them very much. When master is sick we are in great trouble.

7*

Every night the slaves gather around the house, and send up one or two to see how master does. They creep up to the bed, and with a very soft voice, inquire, "How is dear massa? O massa, how we want to hear your voice out in the field again." Well, this is what they say up in the sick room. They come down to their *anxious* companions. "How is the old man?" "Will he die?" Yes! yes! he sure to go this time; he never whip the slave no more. "Are you sure?" "Will he die?" O yes! surely gone for it now. Then they all look glad, and go to the cabin with a merry heart.

Two slaves were sent out to dig a grave for old master. They dug it very deep. As I passed by I asked Jess and Bob what in the world they dug it so deep for. It was down six or seven feet. I told them there would be a fuss about it, and they had better fill it up some. Jess said it suited him exactly. Bob said he would not fill it up; he wanted to get the old man as near *home* as possible. When we got a stone to put on his grave, we hauled the largest we could find, so as to fasten him down as strong as possible.

Who are the patrols? They are men appointed by the county courts to look after all slaves without a pass. They have almost unlimited power over the slaves. They are the sons of run-down families. The greatest scoundrel is always captain of the band of patrols; they are the offscouring of all things, the refuse, the fag end, the ears and tails of slavery; the scales and fins of fish, the tooth and tongues of serpents: they are the very fool's cap of baboons, the echo of parrots, the wallet and satchel of pole-cats, the scum of stagnant pools, the exuvial, the worn out skins of slaveholders; they dress in their old clothes;

they are emphatically the servants of servants, and slaves of the devil ; they are the meanest and lowest and worst of all creation. Like starved wharf rats, they are out nights, creeping into slave cabins, to see if they have an old bone there ; drive out husbands from their own beds, and then take their places. They get up all sorts of pretences, false as their lying tongues can make them, and then whip the slaves and carry a gory lash to the master for a piece of bread.

The rascals run me with their dogs six miles, one night, and I was never nearer dead than when I reached home that night. I only escaped being half torn to pieces by the dogs, by turning their attention to some calves that were in the road. The dogs are so trained that they will seize a man as quick as any thing else. The dogs come very near being as mean as their masters.

Cyrus often suffered very much from these wretches. He was hired with a man named Baird. This man was reputed to be very good to his slaves. The patrols, therefore, had a special spite toward his slaves. They would seek for an opportunity to abuse them. Mr. Baird would generally give his slaves a pass to go to the neighbors, once or twice a week if requested. He had been very good to Cyrus in this respect, and therefore Cyrus was unwilling to ask too often. Once he went out without his pass. The patrols found him and some other slaves on another plantation without any passes. The other slaves belonged to a plantation where they were often whipped ; so they gave them a moderate punishment and sent them home. Cyrus, they said, they would take to the woods, and have a regular whipping spree. It was a cold winter night, the moon shining brightly. When they had got into the woods, they ordered him to take off his outside coat, then his jacket; then he said he had a new vest on; he did not want that whipped all to peices. There were seven men standing in a ring around him. He looked for an opening and started at full speed. They took after him, but he was too spry for them. He came to the cabin where I slept, and I lent him a hat and a pair of shoes. He was very much excited: said they were all around him, but they could'nt whip him. He went over to Mr. Baird, and the patrols had got there before him, and had brought his clothes and told their story. It was now eight or nine o'clock in the evening. Mr. Baird, when a young man, had lived on the plantation of Mr. Logan, and had been treated very kindly by mother. He remembered this kindness to her children. When Cyrus came in, Mr. Baird took his clothes and handed them to him and told him, "Well, boy, they came pretty near catching you." Cyrus put on his clothes, went into the room where the patrols were, and said, "Good evening, gentlemen. Why, I did not think the patrols would be out to-night,—I was thinking of going over to Mr. Reed's; if I had I should have gone without a pass; they would have caught me sure enough. Mr. Baird, I wish you would be good enough to give me a pass, and then I won't be afraid of these fellows." Mr. Baird enjoyed the fun right well, and sat down and wrote him a pass, and the patrols started and had to find the money for their peach brandy some where else.

There were several other times when he had but a hair-breadth escape for his skin. He was generally a little too shrewd for them. After he had outwitted them several times, they offered a premium to any one who would whip him.

How do slaves get information of what is doing in the free States? In different ways. They get something from the waiters that come out into the free States and then return with their masters. Persons from the free States tell them many things; the free blacks get something; and slaves learn most of all from hearing their masters talk.

Don't slaves that run away return sometimes? Yes. There was one returned from Canada very sorry he had run away. His master was delighted with him — thought he had him sure for life, and made much of him. He was sent round to tell how bad Canada was. He had a sermon for the public — the ear of the masters, and another for the slaves. How many he enlightened about the best way to get there I don't know. His master at last was so sure of him, that he let him take his wife and children and go over to Ohio to a camp-meeting, all fitted out in good style, with horse and wagon. They never stopped to hear any preaching, till they heard the waves of the lakes lift up their cheerful voices between them and the oppressor. George then wrote an affectionate note to his master, inviting him to take tea with him in Canada, beyond the waters, the barrier of freedom. Whether the old people ever went up to Canada to see their affectionate children, I have not learned. I have heard of several instances very much like the above.

If the slaves were set free, would they cut the throats of their masters? They are far more likely to kill them if they don't set them free. Nothing but the hope of emancipation, and the fear they might not succeed, keeps them from rising to assert their rights. They are restrained, also, from affection for the children of those who so cruelly oppress them. If none would suffer but the masters themselves, the slaves would make many more efforts for freedom. And sooner or later, unless the slaves are *given free*, they will take freedom at all hazards. There are multitudes that chafe under the yoke sorely enough. They could run away themselves, but they would hate to leave their families.

Did the slaves in Kentucky hear of the emancipation in the West Indies? They did, in a very short time after it took place. It was the occasion of great joy. They expected they would be free next. This event has done much to keep up the hopes of the slave to the present hour.

What do slaves think of the piety of their masters? They have very little confidence in them about any thing. As a specimen of their feelings on this subject, I will tell an anecdote of a slave.

A slave named George, was the property of a man of high standing in the church. The old gentleman was taken sick, and the doctor told him he would die. He called George, and told him if he would wait upon him attentively, and do every thing for him possible, he would remember him in his will: he would do something handsome for him.

George was very much excited to know what it might be; hoped it might be in the heart of his master to give him his freedom. At last the will was made. George was still more excited. The master noticed it, and asked what the matter was. "Massa, you promise do something for me in your will. Poor niggar! what Massa done for George?" "O George, don't be concerned; I have done a very handsome thing for you, such as any slave

would be proud to have done for him." This did not
satisfy George. He was still very eager to know what it
was. At length the master saw it necessary to tell George,
to keep him quiet and make him attend to his duty.
" Well, George, I have made provision that when you die,
you shall have a good coffin, and be put into the same
vault with me. Will not that satisfy you, George?"
" Well, Massa, one way I am satisfied, and one way I am
not." " What, what," said the old master, " what is the
matter with that?" " Why," says George, " I like to have
good coffin when I die." " Well, don't you like to be in
the same vault with me and other rich masters?" "Why
yes, master, one way I like it, and one way I don't."
" Well, what don't you like ?" " Why I afraid, Massa,
when de debbil come take you body, he make mistake,
and get mine."

The slaves uniformly prefer to be buried at the greatest
possible distance away from master. They are superstitious, and fear that the slave-driver having whipped so
much when alive, will, somehow, be beating them when
dead. I was actually as much afraid of my old master
when dead as I was when he was alive. I often dreamed
of him too, after he was dead, and thought he had actually
come back again to torment me more.

Do you think it was right for you to run away and not
pay any thing for yourself? I would be willing to pay, if
I knew who to pay it to. But when I think it over, I
can't find any body that has any better right to me than
myself. I can't pay father and mother, for they are dead.
I don't owe Mrs. Banton any thing for bringing me up the
way she did. I worked five or six years, and earned more
than one hundred dollars a year for Mr. K. and family,

and received about a dozen dollars a year in clothing. Who do I owe, then, in Kentucky? If I catch one of the administrators on here, I intend to sue him for wages and interest for six years' hard work. There will be a small bill of damages for abuse; old Kentucky is not rich enough to pay me for that.

Soon after you came into Ohio, did you let yourself to work? I did. Was there any difference in your feelings while laboring there, and as a slave in Kentucky?

I made a bargain to work for a man in Ohio. I took a job of digging a cellar. Before I began, the people told me he was bad pay; they would not do it for him. I told them I had agreed to do it. So at it I went, worked hard, and got it off as soon as possible, although I did not expect to get a cent for it; and yet I worked more readily and with a better mind than I ever did in Kentucky. If I worked for nothing then, I knew I had made my own bargain, and working with that thought, made it easier than any day's work I ever did for a master in Kentucky. That *thought* was worth more than any pay I ever got in slavery. However, I was more fortunate than many thought I should be; through the exertions of a good friend I got my pay soon after the work was done.

Why do slaves dread so bad to go to the South — to Mississippi or Louisiana? Because they know that slaves are driven very hard there, and worked to death in a few years.

Are those who have *good* masters afraid of being sold South? They all suffer very much for fear master's circumstances will change, and that he may be compelled to sell them to the "SOUL DRIVERS," a name given to the dealers by the slaves.

What is the highest price you ever knew a slave to sell for? I have known a man sold for $1,465. He was a waiter man, very intelligent, very humble, and a good house servant. A good blacksmith, as I was told, was once sold in Kentucky for $3,000. I have heard of handsome girls being sold in New Orleans for from $2,000 to $3,000. The common price of females is about from $500 to $700, when sold for plantation hands, for house hands, or for *breeders*.

Why is a black slave-driver worse than a white one? He must be very strict and severe, or else he will be turned out. The master selects the hardest-hearted and most unprincipled slave upon the plantation. The overseers are usually a part of the patrols. Which is the worst of the two characters or *officers* is hard to tell.

Are the masters afraid of insurrection? They live in constant and great fear upon this subject. The least unusual noise at night alarms them greatly. They cry out, " What is that?" " Are the boys all in?"

What is the worst thing you ever saw in Kentucky? The worst thing I ever saw, was a woman stripped all naked, hung up by her hands, and then whipped till the blood ran down her back. Sometimes this is done by a young master or mistress to an aged mother, or even a grandmother. Nothing the slaves abhor as they do this.

Which is the worst, a master or a mistress? A mistress is far worse. She is for ever and ever tormenting. When the master whips it is done with; but a mistress will blackguard, scold and teaze, and whip the life out of a slave.

How soon do the children begin to exercise their authority? From the very breast of the mother. I have seen a

8

child, before he could talk a word, have a stick put into his hand, and he was permitted to whip a slave in order to quiet him. And from the time they are born till they die, they live by whipping and abusing the slave.

Do you suffer from cold in Kentucky? Many people think it so warm there that we are safe on this score. They are much mistaken. The weather is far too cold for our thin clothing; and in winter, from rain, sleet and snow, to which we are exposed, we suffer very severely. Such a thing as a great coat the slave very seldom has.

What do they raise in Kentucky? Corn and hemp, tobacco, oats, some wheat and rye; SLAVES, mules, hogs and horses, for the Southern market.

Do the masters drink a great deal? They are nearly all *hard* drinkers — many of them drunkards; and you must not exclude mistress from the honor of drinking, as she is often *drunk* too.

Are you not afraid they will send up and catch you, and carry you back to Kentucky? They may make the *attempt;* but I made up my mind, when I left slavery, never to go back there and continue alive. I fancy I should be a load for one or two of them to carry back, any how. Besides, they well know that they could not take me out of any State this side of Pennsylvania. There are very few in New England that would sell themselves to help a slaveholder; and if they should, they would have to run their country — they would be hooted at as they walked the streets.

Now, in conclusion, I just want to say, that all the abuses which I have here related, are *necessary,* if slavery must continue to exist. It is impossible to cut off these abuses and keep slavery alive. Now if you do not approve of these horrid sufferings, I entreat you to lift up your voice and your hand against the whole system, and, with one united effort, overturn the abominations of centuries, and restore scattered families to each other; pour light upon millions of dark minds, and make a thousand, yea, ten times ten thousand abodes of wretchedness and wo, to hail and bless you as angels of mercy sent for their deliverance.

~~~~~~~~~~

Before closing this pamphlet, I want to put in a few pieces, which give such an accurate description of Slavery, that I can testify to the truth of every word of it. Also, a few pieces of poetry, that have been read to me, and with which I have been particularly interested.

WHAT IS SLAVERY?

John G. Whittier answers, —

The slave laws of the South tell us, that it is the conversion of men into articles of property. The transformation of sentient mortals into "*chattels personal.*" The principle of a reciprocity of benefits, which, to some extent, characterizes all other relations, does not exist in that of master and slave. The master holds the plough which turns the soil of his plantation, the horse which draws it, and the slave who guides it, by one and the same tenure. The profit of the master is the great end of the slave's existence. For this end he is fed, clothed, and prescribed for in sickness. He learns nothing, acquires nothing for himself. He cannot use his own body for his own benefit.

His very personality is destroyed. He is a mere instrument — a means in the hands of another for the accomplishment of an end in which his own interests are not regarded — a machine moved, not by his own will, but another's. In him the lawful distinction between a *person* and a *thing* is annihilated. He is thrust down from the place which God and Nature assigned him, from the equal companionship of rational intelligences — a man herded with beasts — an immortal nature classed with the wares of the merchant!

The relations of parent and child, master and apprentice, government and subject, are based upon the principle of benevolence, reciprocal benefits, and the wants of human society — relations which sacredly respect the rights and legacies which God has given to all his rational creatures. But SLAVERY exists only by annihilating or monopolizing these rights and legacies. In every other modification of society, man's personal ownership remains secure. He may be oppressed — deprived of privileges — loaded with burdens — hemmed about with legal disabilities — his liberties restrained. But, through all, the right to his own body and soul remains inviolate. He retains his inherent, original possession of himself. Even crime cannot forfeit it — for that law which destroys his personality makes void its own claims upon him as a moral agent, and the power to punish ceases with the accountability of the criminal. He may suffer and die under the penalties of the law, but he suffers as a *man*, he perishes as a *man*, and not as a *thing*. To the last moments of his existence the rights of a moral agent are his; they go with him to the grave; they constitute the ground of his accountability at the bar of Infinite Justice — rights fixed, eternal, inseparable — attributes of all rational intelligences in time and eternity — the same in essence, and differing in degree only, with those of the highest moral Being — of God himself.

Slavery alone lays its grasp upon the right of PERSONAL OWNERSHIP — that foundation right, the removal of which uncreates the man; a right which God himself could not take away, without absolving the being thus deprived of all moral accountability; and so far as that being is concerned, making sin and holiness, crime and virtue, words without significance, and the promises and sanctions of Revelation, dreams. Hence, the crowning horror of slavery, that which lifts it above all other iniquities, is not that it usurps the prerogatives of Deity, but that it attempts that which even He, who has said "all souls are mine," cannot do, without breaking up the foundations of his moral government. — Slavery is, in fact, a struggle with the Almighty for dominion over his rational creatures. It is leagued with the Powers of Darkness, in wresting man from his Maker. It is Blasphemy, lifting brazen brow and violent hand to Heaven, attempting a reversal of God's laws. Man claiming the right to uncreate his brother; to undo that last and most glorious work, which God himself pronounced good, amidst the rejoicing of the hosts of Heaven! Man arrogating to himself the right to change, for his own selfish purposes, the beautiful order of created existences — to pluck the crown of an immortal nature, scarce lower than that of angels, from the brow of his brother — to erase the God-like image and superscription stamped upon him by the hand of his Creator, and to write on the despoiled and desecrated tablet, "A CHATTEL PERSONAL!"

This, then, is SLAVERY. Nature, with her thousand voices, cries out against it. Against it, Divine Revelation

8*

launches its thunders.   The voice of God condemns it, in
the deep places of the human heart.   The woes and wrongs
unutterable which attend this dreadful violation of natural
justice — the stripes — the tortures — the sunderings of
kindred — the desolation of human affections — the un-
chastity and lust — the toil uncompensated — the abro-
gated marriage — the legalized heathenism — the burial of
the mind — are but the mere incidentals of the first grand
outrage — that seizure of the entire man — nerve, sinew,
and spirit, which robs him of his body, and God of his
soul.   These are but the natural results, and outward demonstrations of slavery — the   crystalizations from the
CHATTEL PRINCIPLE.

It is against this system, in its active operation upon
three millions of our countrymen, that the Liberty party
is, for the present, directing all its efforts.   With such an
object, well may we be " men of one idea."   Nor do we
neglect " other great interests," for all are colored and con-
trolled by slavery, and the removal of this disastrous influence would most effectually benefit them.

Political action is the result and immediate object of
moral suasion on this subject.   Action — action — is the
spirit's means of progress, its sole test of rectitude, its only
source of happiness.   And should not decided action follow our deep convictions of the wrong of slavery ?   Shall
we denounce the slaveholders of the States, while *we* retain *our* slavery in the District of Columbia ?   Shall we
pray that the God of the oppressed will turn the hearts of
" the rulers" in South Carolina, while *we*, the rulers of
the District, refuse to open the prisons, and break up the
slave-markets on its ten miles square ?   God keep us from
such hypocrisy !   Every body, now, *professes* to be opposed

to slavery. - The leaders of the two great political parties
are grievously concerned, lest the purity of the anti-slavery
enterprise will suffer in its connection with politics. In
the midst of grossest *pro*-slavery *action*, they are full of
anti-slavery *sentiment*. They love the .cause, but, on the
whole, think it too good for this world. They would keep
it sublimated, aloft, out of vulgar reach or use altogether,
intangible as Magellan's clouds. Every body will join us
in denouncing slavery, *in the abstract*, — not a faithless
priest nor politician will oppose us ; — abandon *action*, and
forsooth we can have an abolition millenium — the wolf
shall lie down with the lamb — while SLAVERY IN
PRACTICE clanks, in derision, its three millions of un-
broken chains. The Clays, the Van Burens, the Ather-
tons, are all " abolitionists in the abstract." They have no
fear of the harmless spectre of an abstract idea. They
dread it only when it puts on the flesh and sinews of a
practical reality, and lifts its right arm in the strength
which God giveth to *do*, as well as theorize.

As honest men, then, we must needs act; let us do so as
becomes men engaged in a great and solemn cause. Not by
processions and idle parades, and spasmodic enthusiasms,
by shallow tricks, and shows, and artifices, can a cause
like ours be carried onward. Leave these to parties con-
tending for office, as the " spoils of victory." We need
no disguises, nor false pretences, nor subterfuges; enough
for us to present before our fellow countrymen the holy
truths of freedom, in their unadorned and native beauty.
Dark as the present may seem, let us remember with hearty
confidence that Truth and Right are destined to triumph.
Let us blot out the word discouragement from the anti-
slavery vocabulary. Let the enemies of freedom be dis-

couraged ; let the advocates of oppression despair ; but let those who grapple with wrong and falsehood, in the name of God, and in the power of His truth, take courage. Slavery must die. The Lord hath spoken it. The vials of His hot displeasure, like those which chastised the nations in the Apocalyptic vision, are smoking, even now, above its " habitations of cruelty." It can no longer be borne with by Heaven. Universal humanity cries out against it. Let us work, then, to hasten its downfall, doing whatsoever our hands find to do, " with all our might."

Truly your friend,

John G. Whittier.

Hear what Cassius M. Clay says of slavery.

Cassius M. Clay, (nephew of Henry Clay,) has come out in a series of articles in the Lexington (Ky.) Intelligencer, denouncing slavery in unqualified terms—proving that it is the *worst* evil the sun ever shone on — and concluded one of his articles as follows :

"Though no Athenian trumpeter may hurry through the assembled and terrified people in bitter anguish, crying aloud, ' Will no one speak for his country ?', yet from mute and unresisting suffering and down-trodden innocence there comes up a language, no less powerful, to awaken whatever of sympathy and manly indignation may be treasured up in the bosoms nurtured on Kentucky soil,— rich in associations every way calculated to foster all that is just, honest, and true,— without which, chivalry is a crime, and honor but an empty sound ! For them, once more, then, I denounce those who would, by legislation or otherwise, fix the bond of perpetual slavery and the slave trade upon my native State. In the name of those who in all ages have been entitled to the first care and protection of men, I denounce it. In the name of them who, in '76, like those who sent back from Thermopylæ the sublime message, 'Go tell Lacedemon that we died here in obedience to her laws,' illustrated by their blood the glorious doctrines which they taught, I denounce it. In the name of Christianity, against whose every lovely and soul-stirring sentiment it for ever wars, I denounce it. In the name of an advancing civilization, which, for more than a century, has with steady pace moved on, leaving the Cimmerian regions of slavery and the slave trade far in the irrevocable and melancholy past, I denounce it. In the name of the first great law, which at Creation's birth was impressed upon man, self-defence, unchangeable and immortal as the image in which he was fashioned; and in His name, whose likeness man was deemed not unworthy to wear, *I denounce slavery and the slave trade for ever.*"

See *how* they make their ministers, and what kind of ministers they make.

SLAVERY AND CHRISTIANITY.

Sale of human beings for the benefit of Theological education.—The following notice of a public sale is taken from the Savannah Republican of March 3d, 1845. After describing the plantation which was to be sold, the notice adds :—

" Also, at the same time and place, the following negro

slaves, to wit : Charles, Peggy, Antonett, Davy, September, Maria, Jenney, and Isaac—levied on as the property of Henry T. Hall, to satisfy a mortgage *fi. fa.* issued out of Mc Intosh Superior Court, in favor of the Board of Directors of the *Theological Seminary of the synod of South Carolina and Georgia,* vs. said Henry T. Hall.   Conditions, cash.   C. O'NEAL, *Deputy Sheriff, M. C."*

We do not quote this as anything new or strange, but only as *illustrating* a thing of common occurrence.—*Boston Recorder.*

This synod, we suppose, is Presbyterian, with which churches in the free States are in good fellowship relation. Take another case from Zion's Advocate.

Ministers, Hounds, and Runaway Negroes.

The Home Missionary of the Alabama Association, writing to the Alabama Baptist, on the subject of ministerial support, attributes the unwillingness of the people to support their preachers, in part, to the teaching of the anti-missionary ministers.   And he represents one of these riding through the country, with a train of about twenty hounds, and with a brace of pistols, and a Bowie knife projecting out of his pocket, showing a handle which would make a bludgeon, as his informant told him, " large enough to kill the d—l ; and thus fully armed and equipped, he makes his excursions, *hunting runaway negroes !!"*

The Missionary of the Alabama Association goes on to say :—" While it may be right and proper that some one should keep such dogs, and follow such a vocation, we think it does not fitly become the ambassadors of Christ. Let the churches, then, awake to the subject of *Ministerial support."*

That is, so that their ministers may not be obliged to resort to *negro hunting* for a living. Are not these Synods and Associations, "dear brethren?" Now we ask particular consideration to the following, which, if erroneous, we will thank any one to show to be so.

"The highest kind of theft, is that which steals men; and Slavery is nothing less than this. The church which steals them, or holds slaves, which is the same thing, is a thieving church. If that church is in loving fellowship with others, they together form a BROTHERHOOD OF THIEVES."

Of the power of professors of religion over Slavery, Dr. Smith of Virginia thus testifies:—

"I told him, (Dr. Bond,) that Southern Methodists concurred in making the laws, (perpetuating slavery,) voluntarily did so, as far as the system itself was concerned, and that in Virginia, particularly, they could not avail themselves of the benefit of his apology, because so strong is the non-slaveholding interest, that at any time when the membership of the church shall unite their votes with the non-slaveholders in western Virginia particularly, they are competent to overturn the whole system. But that we did not do so, because we considered it our solemn, Christian duty to sanction and sustain the system under its present unavoidable circumstances."

A HARD CASE.— Last week a case was brought up before the Orphans' Court of this county, which must shock the sensibilities of every right-minded man. In 1839 a law was passed to prohibit free blacks from coming into this State from other States, whether to settle or not, under the penalty of twenty dollars for the first offence. If the negro be unable to pay the fine, he is to be committed to jail, and sold as a slave for life. The twenty dollars goes to the informer. In case the negro remains five days in this State after his first conviction, or returns into it after his departure, he is liable to pay a fine of *five hundred dollars*, one half to the informer; and on his inability to pay to be sold for life. After stating the above, we feel it necessary to assure our readers, that this is the forty-fifth year of the nineteenth century, and that this law exists in America, and not in any of the darkened countries of Europe!

Last week, under this law, a negro was brought before the Orphans' Court by a late corporation constable, for having come into this State, being a free negro. The statement of the poor old fellow—for he was old and verging to the limit of his years, with little of the strength of manhood left him — was, that he was removing his family from Virginia into Pennsylvania, having been set free for that purpose, and that he was now on his way through Maryland, simply passing through the State, with no thought of harm, no knowledge of the ferocious toils of the law which hung around him. He was sentenced to pay the fine, and the informer, having consented to remit one half, Mr. Bromett, one of our new Whig magistrates, generously and kindly undertook to raise the money by collection among the citizens of the town, to release the unfortunate old man. He was of course successful in his efforts, and had the exquisite enjoyment of winning blessings from a sorrowful heart, and sending the poor gray headed negro on his way rejoicing.—*Frederick (Md.) Examiner, April* 16.

SLAVEHOLDER'S PARODY.

Come, saints and sinners, hear me tell,
How pious priests whip Jack and Nell,
And women buy, and children sell,
And preach all sinners down to hell,
And *sing* of heavenly union.

They'll bleat and ba, dona like goats,
Gorge down black sheep, and strain at motes,
Array their backs in fine black coats,
And seize their negroes by their throats,
And *choke* for heavenly union.

They 'll church you, if you sip a dram,
And damn you if you steal a lamb,
Yet, rob old Tony, Doll and Sam,
Of human rights, and bread and ham ;
Kidnapper's heavenly union.

They 'll talk of heaven and Christ's reward,
And bind his image with a cord,
And scold and swing the lash abhorred,
And sell their brother in the Lord,
To *hand-cuffed* heavenly union.

They 'll read and sing a sacred song,
And make a prayer both loud and long,
And teach the right, and do the wrong,
Hailing the brother, sister throng,
With *words* of heavenly union.

We wonder how such saints can sing,
Or praise the Lord upon the wing,
Who roar and scold, and whip and sting,

And to their slaves and mammon cling,
In guilty conscience's union.

They 'll raise tobacco, corn and rye,
And drive and thieve, and cheat and lie,
And lay up treasures in the sky,
By making switch and cow-skin fly,
In *hope* of heavenly union.

They 'll crack old Tony on the skull,
And preach and roar like Bashan bull,
Or braying ass, of mischief full,
Then seize old Jacob by the wool,
And *pull* for heavenly union.

A roaring, ranting, sleek man-thief,
Who lived on mutton, veal and beef,
And never would afford relief,
To needy sable sons of grief,
Was *big* with heavenly union.

Love not the world, the preacher said,
And winked his eye and shook his head,—
He seized on Tom, and Dick, and Ned,
Cut short their meat, and clothes, and bread.
Yet still *loved* heavenly union.

Another preacher, whining spoke
Of one whose heart for sinners broke,—
He tied old Nanny to an oak,
And drew the blood at every stroke,
And *prayed* for heavenly union.

Two others ope 'd their iron jaws,
And waved their children-stealing paws.
There sat their children in gew-gaws,—
By stinting negroes' backs and maws,
They *keep up* heavenly union.

All good from Jack another takes,
And entertains their flirts and rakes,
Who dress as sleek as glossy snakes,
And cram their mouths with sweetened cakes,
And this goes down for union.

I AM MONARCH OF NOUGHT I SURVEY.

A PARODY.

I am monarch of nought I survey,
    My wrongs there are none to dispute;
My master conveys me away,
    His whims or caprices to suit.
O slavery, where are the charms
    That " patriarchs " have seen in thy face?
I dwell in the midst of alarms,
    And serve in a horrible place.

I am out of humanity's reach,
    And must finish my life with a groan;
Never hear the sweet music of speech
    That tells me my body's my own.
Society, friendship and love,
    Divinely bestowed upon some,
Are blessings I never can prove,
    If slavery's my portion to come.

Religion! what treasures untold
    Reside in that heavenly word!
More precious than silver or gold,
    Or all that this earth can afford.

But I am excluded the light
  That leads to this heavenly grace ;
The Bible is closed to my sight,
  Its beauties I never can trace.

Ye winds, that have made me your sport,
  Convey to this sorrowful land,
Some cordial, endearing report,
  Of freedom from tyranny's hand.
My friends, do they not often send,
  A wish or a thought after me ?
O, tell me I yet have a friend,
  A friend I am anxious to see.

How fleet is a glance of the mind !
  Compared with the speed of its flight,
The tempest itself lags behind,
  And the swift-winged arrows of light.
When I think of Victoria's domain,
  In a moment I seem to be there,
But the fear of being taken again,
  Soon hurries me back to despair.

The wood-fowl has gone to her nest,
  The beast has lain down in his lair;
To me, there's no season of rest,
  Though I to my quarter repair.
If mercy, O Lord, is in store,
  For those who in slavery pine,
Grant me, when life's troubles are o'er,
  A place in thy kingdom divine.

OUR COUNTRYMEN IN CHAINS.

Our fellow countrymen in chains,
    Slaves in a land of light and law!
Slaves crouching on the very plains
    Where rolled the storm of Freedom's war!
A groan from Eutaw's haunted wood —
    A wail where Camden's martyrs fell —
By every shrine of patriot blood,
    From Moultrie's wall and Jasper's well.

By storied hill and hallowed grot,
    By mossy wood and marshy glen,
Whence rang of old the rifle-shot,
    And hurrying shout of Marion's men!
The groan of breaking hearts is there —
    The falling lash — the fetter's clank!
Slaves — SLAVES are breathing in that air,
    Which old De Kalb and Sumter drank!

What, ho! — our countrymen in chains!
    The whip on WOMAN's shrinking flesh!
Our soil yet reddening with the stains
    Caught from her scourging, warm and fresh!
What! mothers from their children riven!
    What! God's own image bought and sold!
AMERICANS to market driven,
    And bartered as the brute, for gold!

Speak! shall their agony of prayer
    Come thrilling to our hearts in vain?
To us, whose fathers scorned to bear
    The paltry menace of a chain?
    9*

To us, whose boast is loud and long
 Of holy Liberty and Light —
Say, shall these writhing slaves of wrong,
 Plead vainly for their plundered Right ?

Shall every flap of England's flag
 Proclaim that all around are free,
From " farthest Ind " to each blue crag
 That beetles o'er the Western Sea ?
And shall we scoff at Europe's kings,
 When Freedom's fire is dim with us,
And round our country's altar clings
 The damning shade of Slavery's curse ?

Just God ! and shall we calmly rest,
 The Christian's scorn — the Heathen's mirth —
Content to live the lingering jest
 And by-word of a mocking Earth ?
Shall our own glorious land retain
 That curse which Europe scorns to bear ?
Shall our own brethren drag the chain
 Which not even Russia's menials wear ?

Down let the shrine of Moloch sink,
 And leave no traces where it stood ;
No longer let its idol drink
 His daily cup of human blood :
But rear another altar there,
 To Truth, and Love, and Mercy given,
And Freedom's gift, and Freedom's prayer,
 Shall call an answer down from Heaven !

EXTRACT

FROM CAMPBELL'S "PLEASURES OF HOPE."

And say, supernal Powers! who deeply scan
Heaven's dark decrees, unfathomed yet by man,
When shall the world call down, to cleanse her shame,
That embryo spirit, yet without a name,—
That friend of Nature, whose avenging hands
Shall burst the Lybian's adamantine bands?
Who, sternly marking on his native soil
The blood, the tears, the anguish and the toil,
Shall bid each righteous heart exult, to see
Peace to the slave, and vengeance on the free!

Yet, yet, degraded men! th' expected day
That breaks your bitter cup, is far away;
Trade, wealth, and fashion, ask you still to bleed,
And holy men give Scripture for the deed;
Scourged and debased, no Briton stoops to save
A wretch, a coward; yes, because a slave!

Eternal Nature! when thy giant hand
Had heaved the floods, and fixed the trembling land,
When life sprung starting at thy plastic call,
Endless her forms, and man the lord of all!
Say, was that lordly form inspired by thee,
To wear eternal chains and bow the knee?
Was man ordained the slave of man to toil,
Yoked with the brutes, and fettered to the soil;
Weighed in a tyrant's balance with his gold?
No!—Nature stamped us in a heavenly mould!
She bade no wretch his thankless labor urge,
Nor, trembling, take the pittance and the scourge!

No homeless Lybian, on the stormy deep,
To call upon his country's name, and weep!

Lo! once in triumph, on his boundless plain,
The quivered chief of Congo loved to reign;
With fires proportioned to his native sky,
Strength in his arm, and lightning in his eye,
Scoured with wild feet his sun-illumined zone,
The spear, the lion, and the woods, his own!
Or led the combat, bold without a plan,
An artless savage, but a fearless man!

The plunderer came!—alas! no glory smiles
For Congo's chief on yonder Indian isles;
For ever fall'n! no son of nature now,
With freedom chartered on his manly brow!
Faint, bleeding, bound, he weeps the night away,
And when the sea-wind wafts the dewless day,
Starts, with a bursting heart, for evermore
To curse the sun that lights their guilty shore!

The shrill horn blew; at that alarum knell
His guardian angel took a last farewell!
That funeral dirge to darkness hath resigned
The fiery grandeur of a generous mind!
Poor fettered man! I hear thee whispering low
Unhallowed vows to Guilt, the child of Wo!
Friendless thy heart; and canst thou harbor there
A wish but death—a passion but despair?

The widowed Indian, when her lord expires,
Mounts the dread pile, and braves the funeral fires!
So falls the heart at Thraldom's bitter sigh!
So Virtue dies, the spouse of Liberty!

FROM THE SOUTH.—READ! READ!

The following extract is from a long letter written me from a lady living in East Florida, who is an extensive slaveholder, her husband owning two hundred or three hundred slaves. The letter is confidential, and of vast importance ; more especially to protestants. The original will be in my possession. At any time, when it may be wanted to prove the authenticity, you can have it.

W. H. Houck.

"Slavery, I think, is one of the most abominable institutions that the wickedness of man ever invented. I can see no justice in one mortal appropriating the labor of another to his sole use and benefit; slavery demoralizes the whites as well as the blacks. But where there is so much hard work, there is not so much time for committing iniquity among the blacks, as among the whites. It demoralizes the latter, by fostering the passions, causing laziness, bad temper, giving an incentive for the love of dictation, and other base things, which would not be very modest to mention here. I could mention several gentlemen whom I know, who have black wives, unmarried as well as married. Children are raised here with the idea that negroes are put here for the express purpose of contributing to the enjoyment and indolence of themselves. They think it almost a sin to get a horse or a drink of water, if there is a negro in hearing of the voice. It makes no difference how much fatigued the poor creatures are, they must start at the beck.

"Slavery blunts every sympathetic feeling of the human heart. From their infancy children are accustomed to see slaves tied up and cut to pieces. You know that a common whipping is from thirty to forty lashes on the skin, and it is no uncommon thing for them to get two hundred or three hundred lashes. The blood generally starting after the first half dozen lashes. Many persons instead of whipping, beat them unmercifully.

"There is now an old woman, (here the name is given,) under the charge of the marshal at N——,(the name of the place is given,) who, for whipping a woman, or rather causing her to be whipped to *death*, was before the grand jury last court. The citizens, however, are not willing to sit as jurors on her case, as she is so aged. They do not, will not condemn her. Her children are solicitous that she may be sent to the penitentiary, in order that they may get the property; and had it not been for this, her cause would not, probably, have been noticed. It seems the old mistress had been or was ill, and the said negress was employed to brush the flies and keep them off the patient; by some means the negress hit the mistress in the face with the brush. The following was her punishment:—She was taken out before the door, her arms extended to two trees, being stretched to their utmost, and naked. Two negro women commenced whipping her at eight o'clock in the morning, and with short intervals, whipped until two in the afternoon. She begged her mistress to allow her one drop of water to quench her thirst, and time to pray, as she had been very wicked, and should go to hell unless she could pray ; but all to no effect. She was not allowed to call upon *God*. She was untied at two o'clock, a dead woman. Her *murderer* will no doubt go unpunished. You must have known this *woman*, I should have said devil. It was old Mrs. S——. There are some other horrible circumstances connected with this case which I forbear mentioning, for the want of room.

"As it regards treating negroes well it cannot be done. The law establishes a standard for their treatment. Instance as a part, they get one peck of corn per week, and one or two suits of clothing annually; at the same time have to work hard every day, including Sabbaths very often. There is no preaching in Florida for the benefit of the slaves, unless they attend with their masters, and these are domestics, if any. Then they cannot go inside the church! But let me forbear; I am almost alarmed for what I have already written. If I come North this fall, I will give you my views more fully. Remember, this letter is confidential. Yours, &c., G. S."

True Wesleyan.]

N O T E.

The following facts, in confirmation of the story told on page 52, are from Prof. Upham's treatise on *Disordered Mental Action.*

Under the influence of a morbid sensibility, the mere conceptions of the mind, if they happen to be particularly vivid, may at times impart such an increased activity to the whole or a part of the retina as to give existence to disordered or illusory sights. Disordered action may exist in connection with more than one sense at the same time. Such seems to have been the fact in the case of that remarkable visionary, Blake, the English painter. " Did you ever see a fairy's funeral, madam ? " he once said to a lady who happened to sit by him in company. " Never, sir ! " was the answer. " I have," said Blake, " but not before last night." He then proceeded to state as follows : — " I was walking alone in my garden. There was great stillness among the branches and flowers, and more than common sweetness in the air. *I heard a low and pleasant sound*, and knew not whence it came. At last I saw the broad leaf of a flower move, and underneath I saw a procession of creatures of the size and color of green and gray grasshoppers, bearing a body laid out on a rose-leaf, which they buried with songs, and then disappeared." It would seem from this statement, and from other things which are related of him, that this remarkable person was the subject of disordered auditory as well as visual sensations.

The same principle explains also what is related of Napoleon. Previously to his Russian expedition, he was frequently discovered half reclined on a sofa, where he remained several hours, plunged in profound meditation. Sometimes he started up convulsively, and with an ejaculation. Fancying he heard his name, he would exclaim, "Who calls me?" These are the sounds, susceptible of being heard at any time in the desert air, which started Robinson Crusoe from his sleep when there was no one in his solitary island but himself,—

"The airy tongues that syllable men's names,
On shores, in desert sands, and wildernesses."

THE END.

Acknowledgments

I WAS EXTREMELY PLEASED WHEN PAT SODEN, DIRECTOR OF THE University of Washington Press, informed me that he was interested in publishing my introduction to *Narrative of the Sufferings of Lewis Clarke.* His enthusiasm and support were reflected by every member of his staff, and I am deeply appreciative of their kindness and patience during the entire publication process.

I am grateful for the financial support provided by the V Ethel Willis White Endowment. The availability of this endowment certainly encourages authors to write about the themes reflected within this publication.

I owe a special debt of gratitude to Virginia Clark Gayton, my mother and Lewis Clarke's granddaughter. She related stories about Clarke to me and my siblings from the time we were young children. As a result I was imbued with a sense of pride and gratitude toward Clarke that has grown steadily throughout my life.

Cynthia Gayton, my daughter, has communicated with me continuously by phone and email over the past three years about her great-great-grandfather. As a practicing attorney in the District of Columbia and adjunct professor at George Washington University, her research and editing skills have helped me immensely over the course of the project. Some of the most enjoyable of our long telephone discussions have been speculative in nature, regarding the motivations behind significant decisions made by Clarke and the key figures who influenced his life. Those conversations motivated my research and writing. Another rewarding aspect of the conversations has simply been the joy of connecting with my daughter on a regular basis.

I also thank my youngest son, Chandler, a student at Eastern Washington University, for his continual encouragement during the course of this project.

I am forever thankful to the love of my life, my wife—Carmen Walker Gayton. With no apparent angst, she has allowed me to take over our living room and study as repositories for books, periodicals, documents, photographs, and other paraphernalia for my writing projects. Her patience and understanding gave me considerable incentive and the time and space to complete this project.

Carver Clark Gayton, PhD
Seattle, 2012

Further Reading

Compiled by Carver Clark Gayton

Allen, William B. *Rethinking Uncle Tom: The Political Philosophy of Harriet Beecher Stowe*. Lanham, MD: Lexington Books, 2009.

Allison, James. "The Historical Background of Harriet Beecher Stowe's *Uncle Tom's Cabin*." *Evansville (IN) Journal*, April 15, 1881.

Allison, Young E. "'Uncle Tom's Cabin' Lewis Clarke, the 'George Harris' of the Novel, Returns to the Old Farm." *Louisville Courier*, May 16, 1881.

Beason, Tyrone. "We Have a Unique Story to Tell." *Seattle Times*, January 16, 2005.

Child, Lydia Maria. "Leaves from a Slave's Journal of Life." *New York Anti-Slavery Standard*. October 20 and 27, 1842.

Clarke, Lewis Garrard. *Narrative of the Sufferings of Lewis Clarke, During Captivity of More than Twenty-Five Years Among the Algerines of Kentucky, One of the So Called Christian States of North America*. Boston: David H. Ela, 1845.

Clarke, Lewis, and Milton Clarke. *Narratives of the Sufferings of Lewis and Milton Clarke: Sons of a Soldier of the Revolution During Captivity of More than Twenty-Five Years Among the Slaveholders of Kentucky, One of the So Called Christian States of North America*. Boston: Bela Marsh, 1846.

Douglass, Frederick. *Narrative of the Life of Frederick Douglass: An American Slave*. Edited by John W. Blassingame, John R. McKivigan, and Peter P. Hinks. New Haven, CT: Yale University Press, 2001.

Franklin. "Captors Caught." *The Philanthropist*, October 22, 1842.

Fuller, W. P. "A Figure in History, the Career of the Late Lewis Clark." *Detroit Free Press*, February 19, 1898

Fuller, W. P. "Uncle Tom's Cabin: The Original George Harris." *New York Herald Tribune*, July 22, 1870.

Gwathmey, John H. *Historical Register of Virginia in the Revolution, 1775–1783.* Quintin Publications Collection, Genealogical Publishing Company, Inc., 1979.

Hedrick, Joan D. *Harriet Beecher Stowe: A Life.* New York: Oxford University Press, 1994.

"Lewis George Clarke, the Prototype of a Character in 'Uncle Tom's Cabin.'" *Stevens Point (WI) Journal*, August 21, 1896.

Massachusetts Soldiers and Sailors of the Revolutionary War, vols. 1–17. Secretary of The Commonwealth. Boston, MA: Wright and Potter Printing, 1896–1908.

McCullough, David. *1776.* New York: Simon and Schuster, 2005.

Morison, Samuel Eliot, and Henry Steele Commager. *The Growth of the American Republic.* New York: Oxford University Press, 1980.

"Not an Uncle Tom." *Evening Bulletin* (Maysville, KY), December 9, 1895.

"Once a Famous Slave." *Washington Post*, May 12, 1890.

Ripley, C. Peter, et al. *The Black Abolitionist Papers.* Chapel Hill: University of North Carolina Press, 1985.

"She was Little Eva." *Boston Daily Globe*, November 11, 1894.

Stowe, Harriet Beecher. *The Annotated Uncle Tom's Cabin.* Edited by Henry Louis Gates Jr. and Hollis Robbins. New York: W. W. Norton and Company, 2007.

———. *Key to Uncle Tom's Cabin: The Original Facts and Documents Upon Which the Story Is Founded, Together with Corroborative Statements Verifying the Truth of the Work.* London: Thomas Bosworth, 1853.

———. *Uncle Tom's Cabin.* Introduction by Charles Johnson. Oxford and New York: Oxford University Press, 2002.

Taylor, Yuval, ed. *I Was Born a Slave: An Anthology of Classic Slave Narratives.* Vol. 1: 1772–1849. Chicago: Lawrence Hill Books, 1999.

"'Uncle Tom's Cabin': An Interview with Lewis Clark, the 'George Harris' of the Story." *Chicago Tribune*, August 30, 1880.

Vacheenas, Jean, and Betty Volk. "Born in Bondage: History of a Slave Family." *Negro History Bulletin* (May 1973): 101–6.